How to Spit Nickels

And 101 Other Cool Tricks You Never Learned to Do as a Kid!

Jack Mingo

Illustrations by Michele Montez

CONTEMPORARY BOOKS

A TRIBUNE COMPANY

Library of Congress Cataloging-in-Publication Data

Mingo, Jack, 1952–
    How to spit nickels, and 101 other cool tricks you never learned
to do as a kid / by Jack Mingo ; illustrated by Michele Montez.
       p.   cm.
    ISBN 0-8092-3724-5 (paper)
    1. Montez, Michele.   II. Title.   III. Title: How to spit nickels.
GV1547.M55   1993
793.8—dc20   93-25690
                                                        CIP

Written, created, and packaged by MingoMania
Photographs by Robert S. Boni and Fritz Springmeyer
Published by Contemporary Books
An imprint of NTC/Contemporary Publishing Company
Two Prudential Plaza, Chicago, Illinois 60601-6790
Manufactured in the United States of America
International Standard Book Number: 0-8092-3724-5
10   9   8   7   6

TO KIDS OF ALL AGES

Dear Friends,

Welcome to my book. Do come in, but please wipe your feet first.

This book contains tricks, stunts, and other great stuff. Some are just spontaneous silly things you can do right now with things you have on hand. Others are more complicated and take preparation and practice.

I wrote this book for grownups who want to play like kids again. When I look at adults, a lot of us seem to be sad, serious people who can't remember back to the time when we thought we'd never grow up.

How did we all get so *serious*? And how can we learn to be playful again? Well, this book can be a start, sort of a 102-Step Program for Recovering Adultaholics.

Even though I wrote this book with grownups in mind, most of the tricks can be done by anybody.

But be forewarned, kids and adults: A few of these tricks involve things like matches or knives. Please make sure a

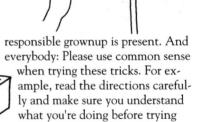

responsible grownup is present. And everybody: Please use common sense when trying these tricks. For example, read the directions carefully and make sure you understand what you're doing before trying something new.

I hope you have fun with these tricks.

Your special pal,

Jack Mingo

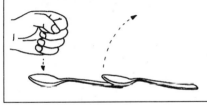

CONTENTS

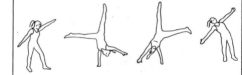

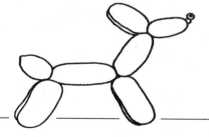

SPECIAL THANKS

Nuna Mingo

Elana Mingo

Fritz Springmeyer

Bob Boni

John Javna

Gene Brissie

Jessica Mingo

Ken Taylor

Emma Lauriston

Chanel Ortman

Stefano Boni

Caci Boni

George Capps

Roger Mingo

Susan Jackson

Becky Welch

Paul Mingo

Joanne Miller

Lenna Lebovitz

Pam Davis

Cecelia McLean

Ms. Lee & "Grandma Helen," Otis
  Elementary School Library

Alameda (CA) Public Library

Berkeley Public Library

Oakland Public Library

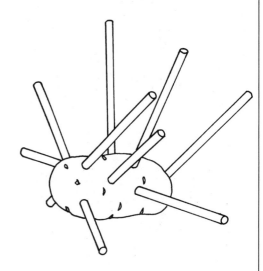

FOOD TRICKS

Food can be more than mere nourishment—it can be fun, too.

Following are several tricks and stunts, all having something to do with food. Most use real food, except for the Giant Eggs, which only *look* like they're real food, albeit unnaturally large.

So forget all those injunctions from your parents against playing with your food. After all, if we were meant to be serious about what we eat, God wouldn't have created such inherently silly foods as spaghetti, Jell-O, watermelons, artichokes, eggplants, bananas, or any of the squishy hot cereals.

SLICE FRUIT IN THE PEEL

Your hapless victim peels a banana for morning cereal—and finds that it comes pre-sliced! What gives? Is this the result of some fiendishly clever genetic engineering?

1 Get a ripe banana, a thin needle, and some thread.

2 Push the threaded needle into a spot on the ridge of the banana, angled along the inside of the peel. Bring it out at the next ridge, leaving a few inches of thread sticking out of first hole.

3 Push the needle back through the second hole, angled toward the next ridge.

4 Keep repeating until you have gone completely around the banana and the needle has come out of your first hole again.

5 Hold both ends of the thread and pull. The thread will pull out through the banana, slicing it cleanly in two.

6 Repeat the process in other spots until you've made several slices. Make sure your victim picks it from the bowl.

Variation: You can also precut an apple, pear or similar fruit under its peel and surprise your friends with a demonstration of your strength.

1 Carefully sew under the skin, as with the banana trick (the needle holes will show so don't let your friends look too closely).

2 Offer half the apple to someone. "Oh, wait. I don't have a knife. Oh well, no matter . . ."

3 With a slight twist of your hands, you break the apple cleanly in half.

FIND A DIME IN A LIME

You show a fresh, unmarked piece of fruit—almost any fruit—to your friends and ask if it looks unusual to them.

"Funny thing," you say vaguely. "I have a strange feeling about this. It has a peculiar scent." You pull out a knife and cut the fruit in half. Inside, there's a dime!

"I *told* you it had a peculiar scent," you say. "Well, actually it was more like *ten* scents."

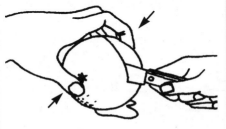

How You Do It

1 Pick out an unblemished piece of fruit. Make sure there are no holes, cracks, or slits that would allow your friends the comfort of thinking you slid a dime in.

2 Using rubber cement, stick a dime on the blade of the knife. Look at the other side of the blade and make sure that the dime isn't visible. Let the glue dry. When you display the knife, show only the dimeless side, of course.

5 When you get halfway through the fruit, squeeze the fruit so that the coin falls off inside.

MAKE ROCK CANDY

Rock candy looks a lot like quartz or some other crystalline rock, yet tastes like sugar. There's a reason for that. Rock candy actually *is* crystalized sugar.

If you look closely at sugar, you'll see that it is made up of tiny cubes. When you make rock candy the tiny crystals dissolve and then reform into similar but much larger crystals. The process and results are pretty impressive, although awfully slow.

1. Fill a tall drinking glass with white sugar.

2. Bring a small panful of water to full boil.

3. Begin pouring the hot water into the sugar, stirring constantly until the sugar is completely dissolved and the glass is full of the hot, clear sugar solution.

4. Tie a clean paperclip to a clean piece of white string, and lower it into the sugar solution until it almost reaches the bottom of the glass. Tie the string to a pencil, which you rest on the lip of the glass.

5. Put the uncovered glass in a warm place where it won't be moved or disturbed. Wait for a few days.

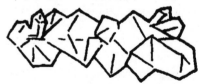

6. Crystals will begin growing on the string. They will also form a crust on the surface, which you want to break so water can evaporate. When the crystals stop growing on the string, remove the candy, let it dry, and share it with a friend.

MAKE DOZENS OF GIANT EGGS

My brother Roger and I came up with these giant Mingo Eggs decades ago when we were both in school. Since then we've made thousands of them for fun, friends, art galleries, and store window displays.

The eggs themselves can be made any size from about 4" in diameter to about 12". Since the eggs are fragile and hollow, we suggest starting with the smaller size. The bigger they are, the easier they break.

What You'll Need

- Large plastic basin
- Square plastic food container
- Plaster of paris
- Stirring stick

- Large clean plastic squeeze bottle
- Egg-shaped balloons
- Small knife or scissors

How You Do It

1 The most important step is to find balloons that are shaped like eggs. Get together your supplies before you start because once you mix the plaster you don't have much time.

2 Find a place where water and flying plaster won't do much harm. Prepare for a mess. Wear old clothes, put down plastic or newspapers, and work outdoors if you can. Fill your plastic basin with clean water.

3 Fill a square plastic storage container half-full with water. Begin adding plaster, stirring continu-ously until it reaches the consistency of a thin milk shake. Now you have to work quickly, because the plaster will set within 5 to 10 minutes.

4 Pour the plaster into your squeeze bottle. Pouring out of the corner of your square container, you'll only spill a little if you approach the problem with a steady hand and an insouciant attitude.

5 Put your first balloon on the mouth of the squeeze bottle as if you were making a water balloon on a faucet.

6 Turn the bottle upside down. Hold the neck of the balloon so it doesn't slip off the bottle. Squeeze plaster into the balloon, inflating it to about the size of a tangerine.

7 Take the balloon off the bottle, squeezing its neck so the plaster doesn't escape. Blow it up the rest of the way (if you don't like plaster in your mouth, use a straw) and tie it off. Float it in the water tub.

8 Repeat steps 5, 6, and 7 until you run out of plaster. Quickly clean your bottle before the leftover plaster hardens.

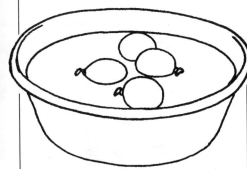

9 Gently turn the balloons, end to end, smoothly coating their insides with plaster, until the plaster stops moving and a heavy side develops. You'll feel it. *Immediately* stop turning the balloons and let them float untouched for at least 10 minutes.

10 When the plaster has completely hardened, cut the balloon away with your blade, being careful not to gouge the surface.

11 Trim away excess plaster from the "navel" where the neck was. And there you have it. No yolk! A giant egg!

GRAPE THROUGH YOUR HEAD

Here's what the trick looks like. You pick up a grape from a fruit bowl and suddenly slam it against your head. After a short pause, it pops out of your mouth.

1 Put a grape in your mouth when nobody's looking. To cover your tracks, pretend to chew and swallow.

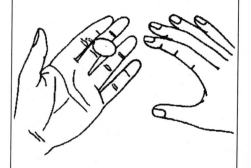

2 In your left hand, take another grape with a small amount of stem attached. Pinch the stem firmly between the joints of your first two fingers. Say something attention-grabbing like "Hey, take a look at this grape" or even "Death to the zinfandel!"

3 Cup both your hands and casu-ally pretend to pass the grape to your right hand, but keep holding by the stem so it stays in your left hand.

4 Quickly slap your right hand (which everyone thinks has the grape) onto the top of your head and hold it there. Make an alarmed face, then relax.

5 Wait for a few seconds, take your hand away, and suddenly pop the grape out of your mouth. Smile sweetly and go on with your business.

FIRE TRICKS

These tricks have been selected as ones that a reasonable person can and will do safely (our ever-prudent lawyers suggested we leave out some of the questionable ones like Breathing Fire, Fun with Napalm, Life's a Bang with Plastic Explosives, and the ever-popular Walking on Hot Coals).

On the other hand, if fire tricks are abused or undertaken carelessly, there is always a potential for bad consequences. (That, by the way, is true of *all* of the tricks in this book, not to mention *life itself*.) Fire should be used with all due caution, adult supervision, and respect for all potential dangers.

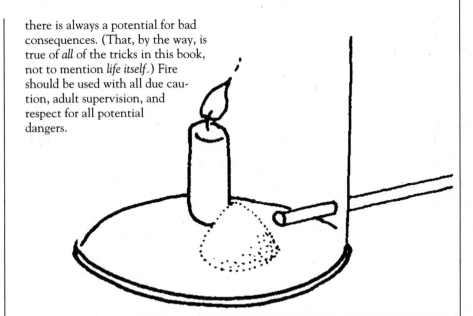

SLEEVE EXTINGUISHER

You light a match with your right hand and hold it up for all to see. You blow into your left sleeve and the match in your right hand goes out.

How You Do It

1 The joke only works if you're wearing long sleeves (otherwise, you have to blow into your pant leg, a much more difficult procedure).

2 Light a wooden match in your right hand, holding it loosely between your middle finger and thumb.

3 After a few moments, but before the flame gets too big, lift your left arm and take a deep breath.

4 Blow hard into your sleeve. Be convincing— let people wonder afterward if it might really be possible to blow out the match in this way.

5 As you blow, bring your right index finger forward and give the match a hard flick with your fingernail, just above your thumb.

6 Your quick flick will extinguish the flame instantly and inexplicably.

SMOKING FINGERTIPS

Did you know that the striking surface of matchbooks contains a type of red phosphorus that ignites at a low temperature? You can release this compound and make a harmless plume of smoke appear from your fingertips. Here's how.

1 Get a metal pan and a couple of matchbooks and get to a place away from wind, burnables, or your smoke detector.

2 Rip the striking surface—that rough thing you rub the matches on to light them— from one of the matchbooks. Place it *facedown* on the metal pan, striking surface resting on the pan.

3 Take the other book of matches and light the cardboard surface. Let it burn and smolder in the pan.

4 When it's done burning, you'll notice that a reddish brown residue has collected on the pan surface. This is a phosphorus compound, set free from its cardboard prison. Rub your finger and thumb in it.

5 When you rub your finger and thumb together, the warmth from the friction is high enough to "burn" the chemical without hurting you. Smoke will curl from your fingertips. Amazing!

TWO OTHER FIRE TRICKS

"Safety Match" Dollar

Have you ever gotten stuck with safety matches—but no striking surface? (This will happen if you do the previous trick a lot.) "Throw them out," you say. "Everybody knows that safety matches will only start on the striking surface. That's why they're called safety matches."

Well, true. With the exception of one common item.

Money. Paper bills, to be exact. Take a crisp dollar bill and scratch a safety match across the length of it. It won't work on anything else we've tried, but a new bill, yes. Why? Frankly, we don't know.

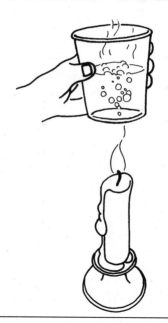

Boil Water in Paper

Quiz: What happens if you fill a paper cup with water and put a candle flame up to the bottom?

a. The flame will go out.

b. The cup will burn.

c. The water will eventually boil.

d. The planets will shift and universal peace will come to all lands.

The correct answer is c. To make fire, you need three things: fuel, oxygen, and enough heat. The water absorbs heat so quickly that the cup never gets hot enough to burn. The water will boil, but the cup won't burn unless you wait until the water has boiled away.

FLOUR POWER BLOWS THE LID OFF

This is the coolest trick I ever learned in high school physics. You blow lightly into a straw poking out of a large canister, and a split second later, the top blows off!

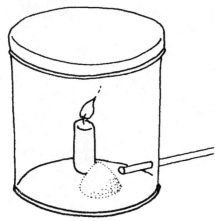

1. Get a metal canister with a top that easily slides on and off (not a screw-on lid).

2. Make a straw-sized hole in the side, about an inch from the bottom. Stick a straw a few inches into the hole.

3. Stick a candle on the bottom of the canister. Put a small pile of flour directly in front of the straw inside the canister.

5. Find a good spot to do this, like outdoors. Light the candle and put the lid on.

6. Blow into the straw. If you set up everything right—*KA-BOOM!* The lid'll blow off with an impressive amount of fire and smoke.

Note: Flour doesn't burn well in a pile (try it!), but it will when atomized into a cloud. Flour mills and saw-mills have to be constantly on guard to keep dust levels down and flames away. Otherwise, this same thing can happen—in a big way.

POW!

GYMNASTICS

Cartwheels & Stands

Certain gymnastics are as impressive as anything and not that difficult with practice. We're talking about such old crowd pleasers as headstands, handstands, and cartwheels, as well as lesser known things like the horizontal handstand, the double forward roll, and the knee walk.

As with most things physical, being in good shape improves your chances of success. As always, play it safe and try these out with appropriate levels of precaution, padding, and clearance.

HEADSTANDS

The Classic Headstand

1 Squat on a mat or very soft lawn with plenty of falling room in all directions. Place your hands on the ground, spread as wide as your shoulders. Put your head on the ground, about 10" in front of your hands.

2 Lift your knees and rest them on your elbows in what we used to call "the toad stand."

3 Lift your legs slowly until they are straight up. Arch your back slightly and point your toes. If you want some support while you learn, do this with someone holding you up, or against a wall.

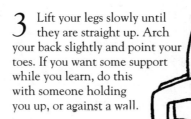

Yoga Headstand

This is a cooler, slightly harder headstand variation.

1 Clasp your hands behind your head. Place your forearms on the mat with your elbows and head forming the triangle.

2 Push off the ground quickly with first one foot and then the other; raise both legs until they are straight up in the air.

HANDSTAND

If you can get the headstand, there's a good chance you can get the handstand. You may want to start out against a wall until you get the feel for this.

1 Get into the racer's start stance you see in track and field events:

one foot forward and bent; the other straight and back; both hands on the ground 12" to 24" ahead of your front foot.

2 Lock your arms straight. Focus your eyes on the mat between your hands.

3 In quick succession, kick up your back leg

and then your front—up into the handstand position. It will take a few tries, so this is a good time to practice falling gently.

4 It is the ends of your fingers that keep you balanced—if you're falling backward, push with your fingertips until you've regained balance; if falling forward, release your fingertip pressure.

HORIZONTAL HANDSTAND

This one is called the Peacock in yoga circles, I'm told. You balance on your hands with your body held parallel to the floor. It doesn't take much strength, but strong stomach muscles help.

1 Get down in a crawling position on the floor, with one difference: position your hands *backward* with your fingers pointing toward your feet.

2 Slide forward so your stomach rests on your elbows. Straighten your body.

The weight of your legs keeps your toes on the floor, your head inclined upward.

3 But now we change that. Push off gently with your toes, lean your head forward, and angle your

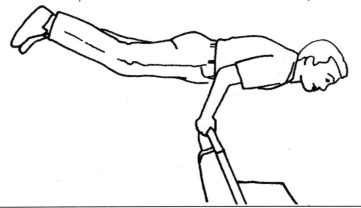

arms forward to move your center of gravity forward. Move gently and slowly, so you don't shift too quickly and bang your nose against the floor.

4 Your toes and knees will slowly lift off the ground. Arch your back and hold yourself parallel to the ground. Amazing!

5 Once you get good at this, you can easily perch like a bird on the back of a couch or anywhere else that will support your two hands and body.

CARTWHEEL

1 Begin in a standing position. Face forward. If you're right-handed, extend your left leg and arm.

2 The next steps happen in about a second, so visualize, practice, and get the sequence right before trying for real.

3 Step forward onto your left foot while reaching down to the mat with your left arm.

4 Kick your right leg up and over your head. It helps to visualize this movement as kicking up to a handstand sideways.

5 Push off the mat with your left leg. Place your extended right hand onto the ground, shifting your weight off your left hand and onto your right.

6 Drop your right foot to the mat, followed by your left foot.

7 During all this, try keeping your arms and legs straight and in the same flat plane, as if they're spokes in a wagon wheel.

TWO-PERSON FORWARD ROLL

Most people can do a simple forward roll, but this is twice the fun because you do it with another person. If you have a long expanse of lawn, two people can roll merrily along for quite a while.

1 Have your friend lie on his or her back.

2 You stand with your feet straddling your friend's head, facing him or her.

3 Your friend puts both feet in the air. Reach out and grasp your friend's ankles, and have your friend grasp yours.

4 Hold on tight and push gently with your toes as if you were diving into a pool. You will begin rolling forward and down. Your weight will begin lifting your friend up off the ground. You will look like a big wheel.

5 Tuck your head forward so that your shoulders gently contact the ground.

6 Keep going until you are in your friend's original position and vice versa. Now it is your friend's turn to push off and continue the roll.

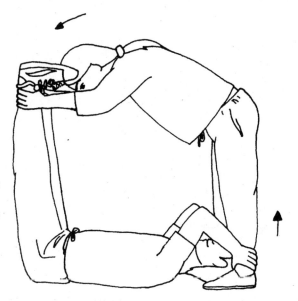

KNEE WALK

If you get a room full of people doing this together, the effect is very funny. Their proportions change and they stagger around in a stiff-legged gait, now and again pausing to fall over. It is sort of like walking on stilts, but you get shorter instead of taller.

1 Find a soft carpet or a stretch of grass. Keep far away from anything fragile, sharp, hard, or messy, since you will probably fall down.

2 Get down on your knees. Reach back and grasp your ankles. Bend your knees and hold your feet up against your buttocks so you balance on your knees.

3 If you just stand there, you'll fall over. Shift from knee to knee to keep from falling (like balancing on stilts).

4 Try walking forward. It's a little hard at first, especially when you're laughing.

5 As you get better at balancing, try other tricks like "kicking" one knee up. It's not too easy.

6 If you enjoy chaotic competitive sports like demolition derbies, try a chicken fight. The goal is to make your friends lose their balance without losing yours. Players are out of the game if they fall over or let go of their ankles.

BALL TRICKS

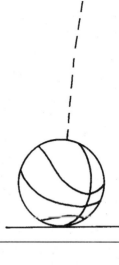

The first ball was probably a rock. Later, legend has it, ball sports began when an army on horseback invented an early form of polo with the heads of vanquished opponents.

Eventually, people discovered that animal bladders could be inflated and tossed around to great general amusement. This led inexorably to professional sports, multimillion-dollar contracts, the Super Bowl, and a general decline in using balls purely for the fun of it.

But it's not too late. Here are some delightfully pointless things to do with balls. And, best of all, you don't even have to cut off somebody's head first.

Launch a Ball

1 Find yourself a tennis ball and a properly inflated basketball.

2 Stack the tennis ball directly on top of the basketball.

3 Carefully drop the balls so that they stay together. Step back!

4 The basketball will stop dead on the ground. The tennis ball will shoot straight up into the air.

LEAPING HALF-BALL

Unexpected action and noise—just the thing to drive your loved ones crazy. That's the appeal of this trick: the half-balls suddenly leap into the air with a bang.

How You Do It

1 Find a handball, tennis ball, or some other hollow rubber ball. You can recycle old balls that have lost most of their bounce. Handballs give a satisfying leap because their rubber is especially thick.

2 Half a ball! Take a knife or coping saw and carefully cut the ball in half.

3 Turn one of your ball halves inside out and place it, dome up, on a solid surface away from breakables. Wait.

4 The inverted ball sits for anywhere from 5 to 60 seconds and then, without warning—POP!—it jumps into the air. Don't lean over it while you wait, and keep children and pets away—you don't want the ball to hit anybody in the eye.

5 If it jumps too late, like never, turn it right side out again and squeeze it for a while. Try again. If that doesn't fix the problem, pinch and tie it overnight to give it more spring.

6 If it jumps too soon, like before you can put it down, follow the previous advice, but squeeze it *inside out*. If that doesn't work, try tying it that way overnight.

BASKETBALL FINGER SPIN

Have you ever wanted to be able to spin a basketball on your finger? Haven't we all? You, too, can be a spin doctor, even a spinned-ball wizard, if you know the secret.

How You Do It

1 Hold the ball at eye level on your fingertips. Rotate your wrist so that you're looking at the back of your hand.

2 Throw the ball up and spin it at the same time. Spin it as vigorously as you can, but don't throw it more than a few inches up.

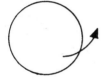

3 Catch the ball at its "South Pole" with your outstretched

finger. Pull your hand down at contact to keep the ball from bouncing off your finger.

4 Balance the ball by watching the *top* of the ball. Imagine a rod running through the ball from your finger: keep the imaginary rod pointing straight up. To speed the ball's spin, use your free hand to gently brush the ball toward you at or below its equator.

ROLL YOUR OWN

Rolling a ball down one arm and up the other is a favorite trick of show-offs everywhere, whether they go with the popular shoulder roll or the less-used chest roll.

3 Catch the ball in the palm of your other hand. Send it back the way it came, or by way of your shoulders.

Chest Roll

1 Hold the ball on the fingertips of one hand. Stretch your arms out and keep your palms up.

2 Start the ball with a slight fingertip flip, arch your back, hold out your chest, and keep your chin out of the way. Lean slightly to give the ball a downward ramp.

Shoulder Roll

1 Balance the ball on the *back* of your hand this time. Steady it by arching your fingers and thumb backward.

2 Hold your arms out, lean your head forward, and try to create a ramp across your shoulders. Lift your hand, lean slightly, and let the ball roll.

3 Catch the ball on the back of your other hand. Steady it by lifting your thumb and little finger.

4 Roll the ball back to your other hand.

33

ANTIGRAVITY TRICKS

Who ever told you you don't understand the gravity of the situation? Gravity is a drag, man—all it does is try to bring you down.

Antigravity tricks are a staple of magicians' acts. They are also used quite often by people claiming to have extraordinary powers. One very famous-name "psychic," who used magicians' tricks to impress a lot of people in the credulous 1970s, actually used the hoary old One-Finger Lift trick as a demonstration of his amazing powers.

You can, too. Just remember that what goes up must come down. So be careful that your pride about defying gravity doesn't lead to a fall.

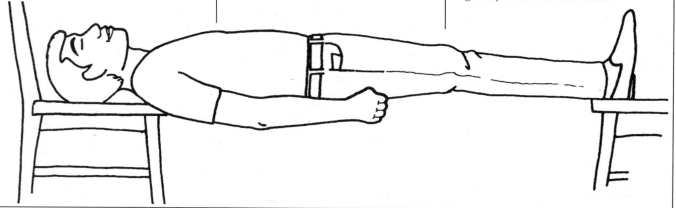

WEIGHTLESS ARMS

L et's start with an easy one you can do by yourself.

2 Bring your arms up until the backs of your hands are touching the door frame. Push hard against it and count slowly to 20.

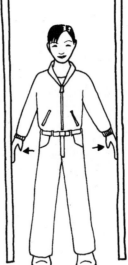

1 Stand in the center of a doorway, arms at your sides.

3 Relax your arms completely and step out of the door frame. Your hands will rise by themselves up into the air!

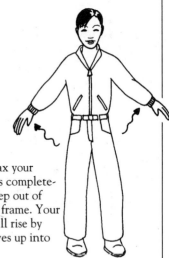

ONE-FINGER LIFT

This one is an old trick—a *really* old trick. "This is one of the strangest things I have ever heard," British diarist Samuel Pepys wrote in 1665, describing this stunt done for fun by French schoolgirls.

Since Pepys's time, it's been used by kids and camp counselors—and by various "psychics" to "prove" their powers. Get five people together and you can be telekinetic, too.

1 Choose the one to be levitated. It helps if he or she is spiritually evolved (just kidding—choose anybody).

2 Tell the levitee to sit down. Have the four others stand, one at each corner of the chair.

3 Tell the lifters in the back to place just their index fingers under the arms of the levitee and the ones in the front to do the same under the person's knees. Tell them to lift.

4 They'll struggle, but the levitee will most likely stay firmly planted on the chair.

5 Now comes the Secret Powers part. Do some gesturing over the person and have him or her meditate about

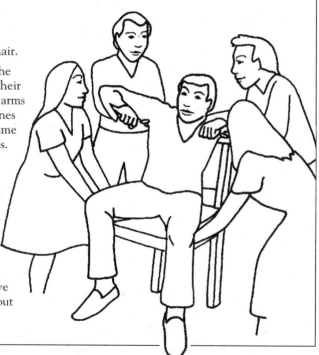

the Incredible Lightness of Being.

6 Have everyone chant mystic chants to get in the mood of believing they can do it. Pepys's French schoolgirls used *"Voycy un Corps mort Royde comme un Baston, Froid comme Marbre, Leger comme un Esprit. Levons te au nom de Jesus Christ* (Here is a corpse stiff as a stick, Cold as marble, Light as a ghost. Let us lift you in the name of Jesus Christ)." You can use it, too—or even the campfire favorite, "O watta goo Siam, O watta na Siam."

7 Everyone returns to lifting position. Tell the levitee to close both eyes, hold arms stiff, and exhale all breath. Tell the lifters to take three deep breaths in unison— on the third, everyone is to lift at once. This time, we have lift-off!

How It Works

Your index fingers are strong—they can hold almost as much weight as your whole hand. And four people lifting the weight of one person is not that big a miracle— as long as they're all lifting in exact unison.

BODY BRIDGE

This is another trick used by magicians and "psychics" to show their powers. You "hypnotize" a volunteer to become as strong and rigid as steel. The subject's body can then easily hold itself up suspended without support between two chairs.

1 Practice it with your subject before doing it in public. Start by placing two folding or kitchen chairs facing each other about 4 feet apart. Place another chair in the center between them to act as a temporary support.

2 Tell your audience about learning the science of hypnotism from a great master in the Mysterious East (East Orange, NJ, that is). Say: "I've been very successful in putting people into deep trances." Ask for a volunteer. Scan the room and then pick the friend you practiced with.

3 Have your subject lie across the three chairs. Make sure he or she is positioned with shoulder blades solidly supported by one chair, feet by the other, and midsection by the center chair.

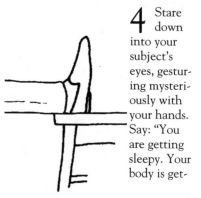

4 Stare down into your subject's eyes, gesturing mysteriously with your hands. Say: "You are getting sleepy. Your body is get-

ting stiffer and more rigid. The more tired you become, the stronger you become."

5 Your friend pretends to nod off. Announce: "The subject is now under my complete control. The subject's body is now as solid as steel."

6 Your subject should keep as straight as possible, arms stiffly held at sides. In your practice ses-sion tell your subject that it helps to grab a small bit of pants leg in each hand and arch the back a little.

7 When it is clear that your friend is stiff and ready, slowly slide the middle chair out. Your friend can bridge the gap in midair.

8 Put the middle chair back and say: "I will count backward from five to one. You will slowly awaken, remembering nothing of what has just occurred . . ." Your volunteer should blink and sit up, swearing that he or she remembers nothing, reacting with disbelief to stories of the strange events.

Note: Believe it or not, most people are strong enough to hold themselves up in this position. However, to be extra safe, use a subject without back, weight, or other physical prob-lems, and try the trick beforehand with cushions in the gap between the chairs.

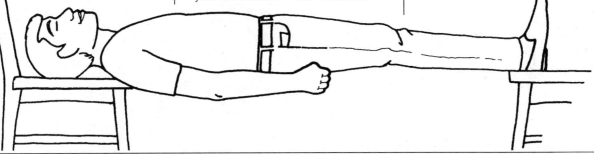

VACUUM LEVITATION

Department stores used to advertise the strength of their vacuum cleaners by using them as antigravity devices—suspending beach balls and such into the air. Impressed kids everywhere begged their parents to let them do the same. Mine never would.

But now I have my own vacuum cleaner, and life is sweet.

1 Tie or tape the inflexible tube of your vacuum cleaner to a kitchen chair, pointing straight up.

2 Attach it via your flexible hose to the hole on the back or bottom of your vacuum—the one that *blows* air instead of sucking it. Turn your vacuum on.

3 Now you can suspend beach balls, Ping-Pong balls, and balloons (weighted with a few paperclips) in the airstream.

4 Best of all, the air wraps around each ball, so you can stack several different things in the same airstream.

5 Hide the vacuum tube and you can make great trick levitation photos (videos are especially effective). Or, take the tube off the chair and walk your balls around the room.

BALLOON TRICKS

Balloons have been providing fun since the days of Joseph and Etienne Montgolfier. On September 19, 1783, they entertained Louis XVI with a 72-foot-high hot air balloon that carried a duck, a rooster, and a sheep. A month later, the brothers launched a person.

English scientist Michael Faraday made the first rubber balloon in 1822, but the toy latex kind didn't appear until 1931. Balloon animals (sometimes called "America's Origami") came along not long after.

Basic Balloon Skills

A lot of people have trouble with balloons, so here's a remedial course.

BLOWING

• Try stretching the balloon before blowing it.

• Use your lungs, not your cheeks. A lot of people end up with dreaded "balloon cheeks"—that prickly pain right in front of the ears—by puffing their cheeks out. Keep them taut, make your mouth an O, and take a deep breath.

TYING

Tying around one finger is hard. Try the two-finger method instead.

• Hold the balloon neck with your left thumb and index finger. Stretch the neck by pushing the rest of the balloon away from you with your right thumb and index finger.

• Keeping the neck taut, wrap it all the way around your right index and middle fingers, then tuck the end of the neck into the crack between them to tie off. The stretched neck and extra slack between the fingers makes tying easy.

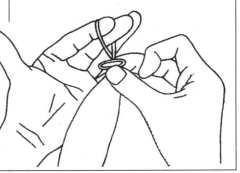

BALLOON ANIMALS

Inflatable Party Animal

Mastering most balloon animals isn't hard. Most of the standard, four-legged types are just variations on the Basic Dog.

1 Find those long balloons. Try a good toy store or check your Yellow Pages under Balloons. If you reach a balloon pro and want to talk the talk, ask for "#260s" (which means 2 inches in diameter, 60 inches long).

2 Inflate the balloon, except for the last 2-3", and tie.

3 Starting at the tied end, pinch the balloon 3" from the knot and twist it a few turns.

2 Twist off two more 3" segments. Fold the balloon on your second twist, and twist together at the first and third. You've just made the dog's nose and ears.

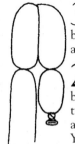

4 Make three more 3" sections and once again fold on your second

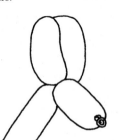

twist and twist together the first and third. You've just made its neck and front legs.

5 The next segment is the dog's body, so make it longer. For its back legs, twist two more 3" sections and leave

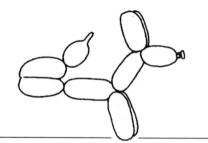

a small bubble at the end for the tail. Once again, bend at the second twist and twist together the first and third. Congratulations! It's a dog!

6 If you're dealing with young kids or other literalists, you can draw on eyes and a mouth. Otherwise, stop here.

A Latex Menagerie

DACHSHUND

Take the basic dog, shorten the legs, and lengthen the body (doesn't this sound like a Monty Python sketch?).

GIRAFFE

Shorten the ears, lengthen the legs a little, lengthen the neck a lot. For literalists, add square spots.

MOUSE

Inflate the balloon only about 12" long and make all segments smaller. Leave the tail long and uninflated.

SQUIRREL

Make it like the mouse, but inflate all of the balloon except 2-3". Give your squirrel a long, inflated tail with an **S** shape. You get the shape by curving and squeezing it until the look is right.

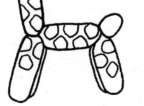

SEW A BALLOON

People will find this surprising—you can stab a needle and thread right through a balloon without popping it.

1 Thread a large needle with bright thread, yarn, or ribbon. A sharp knitting needle or cooking skewer will work, too.

2 Inflate a large balloon only $\frac{3}{4}$ full. Tie it off.

3 Because it is not fully inflated, you can find a thick spot of rubber at the top of the balloon and another near its neck.

4 Take your needle and pierce through the thick rubber near the neck. Quickly push it through the other side. Show your friends that the thread is running right through the center.

5 Don't dawdle—your balloon is leaking air through its two holes. Use the needle to pop it quickly before it noticeably deflates.

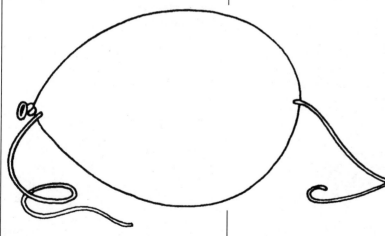

BIKE WITH MOTORCYCLE SOUND

Years ago, kids put playing cards into the spokes of their bikes to make a humming noise when they rode. The sound was totally wimpy.

But there's a way to annoy the neighborhood dogs with a convincing motorcycle sound. It's so good that our testing committee refused to stop taking turns on a 10-speed around our industrial parking lot test site, grooving on the throaty roar. The secret? You use balloons.

1 Any balloon will work . . . for a while. All of them will break, but the really cheap ones may not even make it a hundred yards. Look for balloons with thick walls.

2 Inflate your balloon only part-way—up to the size of a small apple.

3 Tie the balloon's neck around the bar next to your bike's

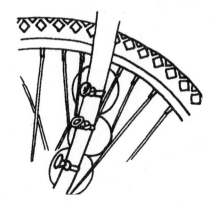

spokes. Push your bike forward to twist the balloon into the spokes to rub under pressure when you ride. Don't back up, or the balloon will pop out again.

4 When you ride slowly, the balloon will sound like an idling "hog": BLUM-*bum-bum*-BLUM. When you speed up, you'll get a roar that can be heard for blocks.

5 If the sound is too wimpy, try wrapping the balloon neck around the bar a second time. Keep in mind, though the live-fast-die-young rule: the louder the noise, the faster your balloon pops.

6 For more noise, put on more than one balloon.

FLY A HOT AIR BALLOON

Watching your own miniature hot air balloon floating soundlessly into the sky can be quite satisfying. Like any activity involving fire, make sure you take all appropriate safety precautions and include at least one responsible adult in your crew. (If none of the adults you know fit that description, try a different trick.)

1 Get 6 sheets of light tissue wrapping paper, any color.

2 Fold each sheet in half, lengthwise. Stack and paperclip them along the edges.

3 On the top sheet draw this pattern along the folds (below, right).

4 Use scissors to cut through all 12 thicknesses of paper, making sure they don't move around as you cut.

5 Unfold your paper. You should find yourself with 6 identical, symmetrical pieces.

6 Start with your top piece and run a thin line of white glue along your pencil line on one half of the pattern.

7 Take another piece and lay it on top of the first piece. Firmly seal the edges together, making sure there are no gaps where air can escape.

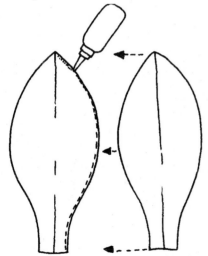

8 Do the same thing with two more pieces, gluing one edge of one to an edge of the other. Do the same again with the last two pieces. You now have three double pieces.

9 Because the tissue paper is so absorbent, the glue will dry fairly quickly. Unfold your three balloon segments. Glue them to each other, edge to edge. The resulting balloon should be a classic hot air balloon shape, complete with an opening at the bottom.

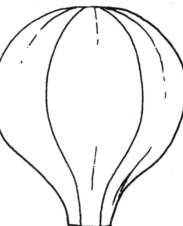

10 When it's dry, gently inflate your balloon with a hair dryer. Patch leaks with glue.

11 Next, assemble your heater unit. Go to the supermarket and buy one of those little cans of fuel (Sterno) used to keep food hot at buffets. Find an empty can in your recycling bin big enough to fit around the Sterno can but small

enough to fit inside the opening of your balloon. Rinse it out, and punch some holes above the bottom rim.

12 You should fly your balloon outside on a cold day with little or no wind. Find a safe, clear, nonflammable place away from trees, houses, and power lines. Bring along some water or a fire extinguisher, to deal with worst case scenarios.

13 Put your burner can on the ground; place the Sterno can inside. Light it through a hole in the burner can's side. Make sure the flames are well contained inside the can before continuing.

14 Hold your balloon over the burner. Lift it slightly to avoid blocking the burner's ventilation holes.

15 After a while, you will feel the balloon trying to lift off the ground. Hold it a little longer until the lift is good and strong.

16 Let go! If everything is right, your balloon will float gently into the air. Get ready to follow it and bring it back when it touches ground.

STRAW TRICKS

Some historians say that the first drinking straws actually were made of straw. Regardless, the first paper straw was designed in 1888 when Marvin Stone wrapped some paper around a pencil and glued it with a watertight glue.

Stone's paper straws imparted a papery, waxy taste and tended to flatten easily, but at least they were environmentally friendly, sort of.

In the 1960s, plastic straws appeared, and it

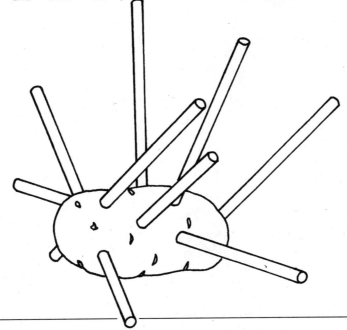

didn't take them long to completely take over to the point where paper straws are now apparently extinct.

Still, plastic straws work for most of the old straw tricks (for example, breaking a camel's back, taking a straw vote, building a straw man). And they've even engendered a few new ones (for example, Pop a Straw, page 50).

So buy a pack of straws (or better yet, raid the closest fast-food restaurant), and let's have some fun.

POP A STRAW

This is a trick that you can do only with certain straws—the cheap transparent ones. Most others are not thin enough.

1 Pinch both ends of a straw so no air can escape.

2 Holding the ends firmly, circle your hands around each other as if they were pedaling a bicycle.

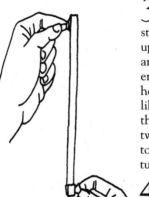

3 Let the straw roll up flat around the ends you're holding, like rolling the end of two tiny toothpaste tubes.

4 Keep winding until the middle of the straw is bulging

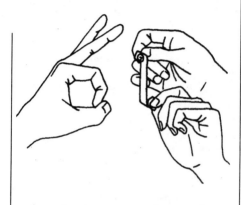

from the air pressure and you can't wind any more.

5 Have a friend finger-flick the middle of the straw *hard*. It'll explode with a modest bang, startling your friends and scaring the horses.

STRAW OBOE

Fast-food restaurants are great places for making noise. There's that cow-with-asthma sound you get by pulling a straw in and out of a plastic drink lid. There's that dying dinosaur sound you get from dragging a styro cup of coffee across formica (this creates a psychedelic wave pattern in the liquid as well). But did you know you can make your own oboe from a plastic drinking straw?

How You Do It

1 Flatten one end of the straw by pinching it.

2 Oboes have double reeds, giving that distinctive sound that's a cross between a mosquito and a Bronx cheer. That's the effect we're going for, too. Cut the corners of your flattened end to create two little reeds.

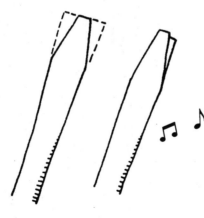

3 Put the reeds in your mouth and blow hard. If you hear no noise the reeds are probably too far apart—try pinching them slightly with your lips as you blow.

4 You want to change the tone? Cut a series of holes each about 1 inch apart. Cover and uncover them with your fingers. Wonderful music! Now all you need is a cobra . . .

STRAW FLUTE

Another instrument for your "orches-straw"—a slide water flute. This is less an instrument that you make than a technique of playing any liquid drink that comes with a straw.

1 Stick the end of the straw an inch or two into the liquid. Hold the straw lightly with your thumb and index finger.

2 Prop your chin on your thumb joint and blow across the mouth of the straw (as if playing a flute or soda bottle). At first it will sound more like wind than a wind instrument, but keep trying until you get a clear, high tone.

3 As you play, move the straw up and down in the liquid. You'll notice that the tone changes. The higher you hold the straw in the water, the lower the tone is . . . and vice versa.

4 Pretty soon you'll learn to control the pitch and be able to play semi-recognizable melodies, like maybe "Turkey in the Straw," "Strawberry Fields Forever," or even "Que Str-Aw Str-Aw."

5 For variety, try the gargling effect made famous by novelty bandleader Spike Jones in the 1940s: stop blowing across the straw and, instead, start humming into it.

TWO MORE STRAW DEALS

Straw Through a Potato

Jab a straw straight through a raw potato? Yes, it's possible, even with a paper straw.

1 Start with a fresh baking potato. Get a good grip on your straw by pinching the end.

2 Now jab the potato at right angles to the surface, using as much force as you can. Be bold!

3 The first few times, you'll probably mess it up—either hitting too softly or at the wrong angle. If you bend your straw, you'll need a new one for your next attempt. How many straws can you get in one potato?

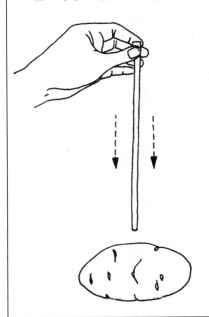

Suck Up a Dime

Can you suck a coin off the table with a drinking straw? That's the challenge for your friends.

1 Start with a dime and work your way up through penny, nickel, quarter, and half-dollar. It gets harder the bigger the coin is.

2 Want an insider's advantage? Sneak a drop of water on the coin. Your suction powers will not be equalled.

BATON TWIRLING

When I was a kid, baton twirling was one of several cool "girl things" (like jacks and rope-skipping) that boys wished they could try without incurring universal scorn. Unfortunately, the gender role pressures were great at the time.

But, hey, these are the 1990s and things have changed . . . somewhat. So for guys (and for those women who were deemed "not the cheerleader type"), we present a course in remedial baton twirling. Get yourself a baton and a spangled outfit, keep your back straight and your head high, lift those knees, keep smiling, and let's twirl!

WRIST TWIRL

This is the basic twirl you do vertically at your side. Like most twirls, it uses a great deal of wrist movement. Change over to the other hand when your wrist gets tired (since you want to be equally good with both hands). Keep your wrist loose, and don't worry that it feels very awkward at first.

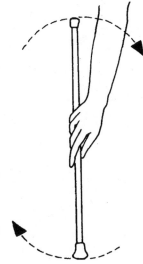

1 Hold the baton centered in your right hand, hanging loosely at your side. Point the "ball" of the baton (the big end) forward and the "tip" (the small end) behind.

2 Tilt your wrist forward until the ball end points straight down. Continue the wrist movement until the ball is behind you and your palm faces away from you.

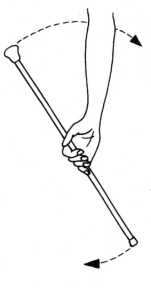

3 Continue the ball up in its circle, and pass it under your arm. End up back in the starting position.

4 Work for a continuous, easy, circular movement. Let your elbow wobble until you develop the loose wrist movement.

FLAT SPIN

The flat spin is done with your arm straight out to the front or side. The baton spins horizontally.

1 Pick up the baton in your right hand with the "ball" on the thumb side of your hand.

2 Hold your arm straight out to your right side at shoulder height, palm facing down. Hold the baton straight out, ball pointing out and tip under your forearm (below).

3 Bend your wrist backward so that your palm is now facing out to the side and the ball is straight back.

4 Bring the ball around to point at your head. Bend your elbow slightly as you turn your palm up (right).

5 Continue rotating your hand until the ball is pointing straight forward and your palm is facing out to the side again.

6 Straighten your wrist and elbow and roll the baton back to its original position.

7 Continue turning, flexing your wrist and elbow. Remember that the ball glides just over your arm; the tip, just under it. Work toward a smooth, continuous circling motion.

FIGURE 8

This is the last of the basic twirls. You do it at waist level in front of you. It's called a Figure 8 because you actually draw a sideways 8 while you do it.

1 Grab the center of the baton, ball toward your thumb, and hold it horizontal at waist level in front of you with your palm down.

2 Dip the ball end down to the left and then flip your hand over to the right so your palm faces up and the ball end flips over, pointing slightly forward and down to the right.

3 Bend your hand so that the tip end points slightly forward and up to the left. Flip your hand over again so your palm faces down again, bringing your hand back to the starting position.

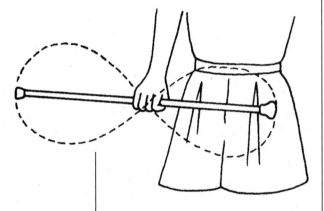

4 Repeat, keeping your arm straight. Relax your hand on the shaft between your thumb and index finger, so that each loop of the figure 8 becomes a twirl.

FINGER TWIRL

This is a nifty piece of dexterity that is as fun to do as it is to watch. You roll the baton up and down your fingers as it twirls.

1 Make a "gun" with your right thumb and index finger. Center the baton between your thumb and outstretched finger and loop them around the shaft (below).

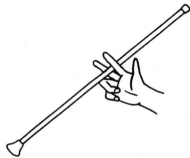

2 Flick your wrist so that the ball swings over to the left. Immediately straighten your middle finger and hold the shaft between your first and second fingers like a cigarette. The ball goes down and to the left.

3 Flick your wrist to the left again and straighten your third finger to catch the baton, which is rolling

across the second finger. The ball end goes up and to the right again.

4 Make one more flick of the wrist, turning your hand all the way over so your palm is facing down. Let go with your little finger at the same time. The baton will roll across the backs of your fingers, landing back between your thumb and first finger where you started. Now do it again, faster!

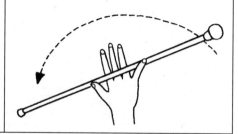

FLIP AND CATCH

One more trick before we put away our sequined leotards.

1 Hold your baton with the ball on your thumb side and your palm down.

2 Begin wth your wrist to the left as far as it will go, and then roll it to the right as far as you can. As your palm turns up, straighten your fingers. Your hand will hit the point where it cannot turn any more, but the baton will continue turning in the **V** of your forefinger and thumb.

3 The ball end, swinging down and to the left, will stop as the shaft catches on your thumb. It'll immediately rebound—up and to the right (see illustration at left).

4 As that happens, throw your hand upward (see above). Let go of the baton with your thumb as you flick your wrist to the left. The baton will—the gods willing—go spinning straight up into the air.

5 Hold your hand palm up, waiting for the baton to come down. Snatch the baton out of the air, going into an immediate twirl.

CARD TRICKS

Hey, hey. *Pick a card, any card.* There's nothing like somebody threatening card tricks to clear most rooms.

The problem with most card tricks is that after a while they all have the same plot—you pick a card and the trickster tells you what it is. If you're lucky, there might be an amusing twist to it (for example, Dial P for Psychic, page 62), but, even then, a few card tricks go a long way.

So a few card tricks are what we give you. Of these, only two resemble the standard "pick a card" variety in any sense—the rest just happen to be tricks you can do using a deck of cards.

Drop Cards into a Hat

Give your friends this challenge: Can you drop cards one by one into a hat from a distance of only four feet? (If you don't have a hat a small box, bowl, or wastebasket will do.)

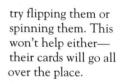

1 Place your hat (or other target) on the floor. Let your friends try first.

2 They will probably fail. Most people will try dropping the cards edgewise—a reasonable approach to the problem, but totally wrong. They may

try flipping them or spinning them. This won't help either—their cards will go all over the place.

3 When it's your turn, carefully hold each card parallel to the floor and drop it so that it stays that way. Try to avoid spinning the card or slanting it.

4 Nine times out of ten, your card will fall right into the target.

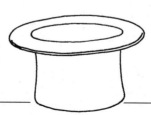

CARDS PITCHER

You throw a loose deck of cards to a spectator. In most cases, the results would be a messy game of "52 Pickup," with cards strewn all over the place.

Unless, of course, you know the secret.

1 Remove a deck of cards from its box, take out the jokers, and shuffle the cards to illustrate that they are not glued, tied, or otherwise connected to one another.

2 Get a volunteer to catch. Have him or her stand back 15 or 20 feet (with practice, you can try 25 feet or more).

3 Hold the deck in your palm with a joker on top and bottom, and the cards squared. The jokers should be pulled back about an inch from the rest of the deck.

4 Using a flat, easy underhand toss, release the pressure on the

jokers, letting the deck slide away from you. The two jokers will stay between your fingers—the rest of the deck will slide through the air in a flat arc, staying intact until they reach your volunteer.

DIAL P FOR PSYCHIC

Tricks involving "mind-reading" can be pretty mind-boggling. But the best we've seen is this one. You mention to a friend that you know somebody who is more psychic than anybody you've ever met. "Let me show you," you say.

Your friend picks any card from a deck and places it faceup. Without leaving the room, you check your address book and give your friend the name and phone number of the "psychic."

Your friend calls. The "psychic" answers, concentrates, picks up the "cosmic vibrations" over the phone, and tells your friend the correct card.

1 First of all, recruit a reliable helper. Make two copies of the tables on the next page. Give one to your helper, and tape the other into your address book.

2 Arrange a time for the trick when your helper will positively be near the phone and prepared.

3 Your friend picks a card from the deck and displays it. You go to your address book to find your helper's phone number. While doing that, secretly check the tables

and find the name that corresponds to the card your friend picked. For example, if your friend chose the 8 of spades and your helper is female, you tell your friend to call "Jessica" at that number.

4 Your friend calls and asks for "Jessica." Your helper says "I am Jessica" and checks the table from the next page. She finds that the name "Jessica" corresponds to the 8 of spades.

5 After a long theatrical pause, your helper announces the right card. Your friend is totally mystified.

Note: No matter how much your friend begs, you obviously cannot repeat this trick.

If Your Associate Is Male

	Diamonds	Hearts	Spades	Clubs
Two	Alan	Arthur	Barry	Byron
Three	Carleton	Charles	Daniel	Dominique
Four	Eduardo	Frederick	George	Gregory
Five	Hampton	Harold	Henry	Jackson
Six	Jason	Jerry	Jonathon	Kenneth
Seven	Kim	Kyle	Lester	Lindsay
Eight	Lyle	Martin	Nathan	Norman
Nine	Oscar	Ogden	Patrick	Paul
Ten	Peter	Pomeroy	Randall	Reginald
Jack	Robert	Roger	Samuel	Seymour
Queen	Sven	Theodore	Thomas	Todd
King	Uri	Virgil	Vladimir	Wadsworth
Ace	Wendall	Wesley	William	Zachary

If Your Associate Is Female

	Diamonds	Hearts	Spades	Clubs
Two	Adrian	Alicia	Anne	Barbara
Three	Brandy	Carolyn	Chanel	Constance
Four	Crystal	Danielle	Deborah	Diana
Five	Donnalee	Elana	Emmaline	Estelle
Six	Flora	Gail	Gloria	Hanna
Seven	Heather	Hope	Jane	Jacqueline
Eight	Jasmine	Jennifer	Jessica	Joanne
Nine	Julia	Kathleen	Kristin	Laura
Ten	Lentil	Linda	Margaret	Maria
Jack	Marianne	Melissa	Nancy	Octavia
Queen	Olivia	Patricia	Penelope	Peony
King	Robin	Shakti	Sharon	Suzanne
Ace	Vanna	Victoria	Virginia	Winifred

JUMPING JACKS

This one's a gas-gas-gas. It looks like the same old card trick again, but it has a good gimmick: the cards supposedly selected by your volunteer—two jacks—jump out of a presealed envelope.

What You'll Need

- 2 stiff cardboard pieces, 3" x 3"
- A big rubber band
- A deck of cards
- An envelope

How You Do It

1 Before your performance, wrap the two pieces of cardboard with the rubber band. This will be the "slingshot."

2 Take out the two red jacks from your deck. Open up the cardboard like a book. Place the two cards on top of the rubber band and "close the book" on them.

3 Holding the cardboard closed, slide the loaded "slingshot" into the envelope with cards aimed upward. Seal it tightly with tape, leaving a little tab to make it easy to open.

4 Take the two remaining jacks and place one on top and one on the bottom of the deck. Put the deck back in its box and the envelope in your pocket. Now you're ready to do the trick.

5 Take your deck out of its box. Invite a friend to cut it anywhere, placing the top half of the deck on the table.

6 Remove the envelope from your pocket. Put it on top of the cards your friend just set down. Have your friend place the rest of the deck on top of the envelope, making a sand-wich.

7 Say: "Earlier today, I sealed two cards in this envelope. If my hunch is

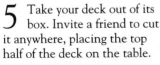

correct, they'll match the cards you just chose when you cut the deck."

8 Ask your friend to read the cards he or she "selected" in the cut—the two cards directly above and be-low the enve-lope (these, of course, are the jacks you put on the top and bot-tom of the deck). Say:

"Please pick them up yourself. I don't want you to touch them because I don't want you to think I'm using sleight of hand or some other trickery."

9 "Coincidentally," the two cards chosen both turn out to be jacks. You say: "No matter. Let's see if my hunch was correct."

10 Open the flap on the enve-lope, squeezing the cardboard inside firmly. When the flap is open, and after you've paused dramatically, loosen your grip. The two cards will shoot into the air.

11 Casually slide the envelope back into your pocket as you pick the two cards up. Show them and say: "There they are, just as I predicted: two jumping jacks!"

CARD PINCER

You can create a set of pincers from a card that will pick up things. This can be done with a playing card, but since it wrecks the card, try a business card instead.

Some business folk use this trick as a way to have a distinctive business card.

But it can just as easily be used to entertain people. Some people have contests to see who can pick up the most weight.

How You Do It

1 Take your card by the two longest edges, your thumb on one side, your middle finger on the other.

2 Squeeze the card with those two fingers while you press the center of the card with your index finger at the same time.

3 The card will fold away from you in a pincer shape. Adjust the folds so your pincers are strong and symmetrical.

4 Start picking up stuff, like salt shakers, silverware, and pens. If you're an amateur ventriloquist, you can paint on a face and talk with your card.

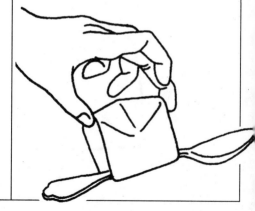

COIN TRICKS

Spare Change?

The first metal coins appeared between 3000 B.C. and 2500 B.C. The Sumerians started smelting them from iron to replace bags of barley (especially valuable to them for beer brewing) as their official legal tender.

Since then, people have had a relationship with coins that is not purely fiscal. The size and shape of coins make them good for screwdrivers, bottle openers, emergency fuses, even decision-making oracles ("flip a coin!").

But the absolutely best use for coins is doing cool stunts.

COAT-HANGER SPIN

This is a stunt that puts the "cent" in centrifuge. A quarter on a coat hanger stays put even when you twirl the hanger around your finger.

1 Check the wire on your hanger to see that it's cut square. Bend the hanger into a diamond shape and hang it upside-down on your finger.

2 Find a place where flying quarters will do no harm.

3 Carefully balance a quarter on the tip of your hanger's hook.

4 After a few swings back and forth, take a deep breath and begin twirling the hanger around your finger. Do this smoothly and confidently and the coin will (often) stay on, because of centrifugal force.

5 Stopping is a little harder. Stretch out your arm and take a step in sync with the swing. Guide the hanger to a swaying stop. Whew!

TWO WAYS TO BALANCE YOUR FUNDS

Dime on a Dollar

Here's a way to balance a dime on the edge of a dollar bill. It's a clever little stunt that doesn't involve trickery.

1 Pull out the crispest bill you have in your wallet. Fold it lengthwise into a sharp edge and stand it up on the table. Challenge your friends to balance a dime on it. They won't be able to.

2 When they give up, fold the bill in half again and put the dime on top of it.

3 Grasp each end of the bill. As you pull your hands away from each other, the coin will balance on the now-straight crease.

Coin Balance on Edge

This balancing trick requires a willingness to cheat.

1 You hold two coins edge to edge between your finger and thumb and challenge anybody to match it.

2 "Match" is right. They won't be able to do it . . . unless they steady the coins with a hidden matchstick, like you're doing.

TWO WAYS TO BLOW YOUR MONEY

Pin Money

1 Take a pin or needle in each hand.

2 Lay a quarter or a dime on the table. Carefully pick it up on its opposing edges with the pins.

3 Blow on the coin. It will spin madly between the two pins, making a noise like a small motor.

Spin Silver from Straw

This is a similar trick using a straw, which can be performed in a restaurant while waiting for your food.

1 Place a penny flat on the table in front of you.

2 Take a soda straw and blow under the penny's edge until the coin jumps up from the table.

3 While the coin is up on its edge, keep blowing. The penny will begin spinning wildly.

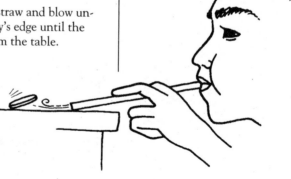

PENNIES FROM HEAVEN

This is a mystifying coin trick that requires no special skill or preparation (although having a flat head helps). A coin disappears into thin air, and then suddenly drops from the sky.

1 Have your friend stand and hold out one hand, palm out. Show a coin and explain that when you count "three" your friend should try to grab it from your hand.

2 Hold the coin just barely sticking out beyond your thumb and first few fingers. Dramatically raise your hand up above your head. Bring it down into your friend's palm and say "One!"

3 Raise your hand again, hesitate deliberately for a moment, and bring it down into your friend's outstretched palm. Count "Two!"

4 Raise your hand again, but this time quickly hide the coin on the

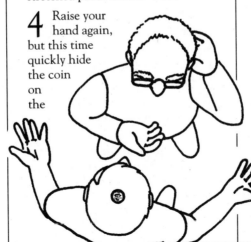

top of your head. Bring your hand down again and say "THREE!"

5 Your friend will grab for the coin, trapping your fingers. But there's no coin there! You shrug and spread your hands wide in mock astonishment, showing that the coin has apparently vanished.

6 Suggest that your friend should look down at his or her palm again and concentrate on making the money come back.

7 After a second, bend your head down slightly so the coin drops off your head into your friend's palm. Look up to the sky in amazement.

COPPERPLATE A NAIL

Here's a way to make some dirty pennies nice and shiny—while at the same time coating a nail with copper.

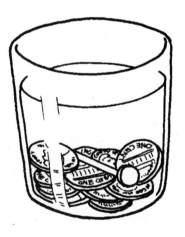

How You Do It

1 Pour $1/4$ cup of vinegar into a glass (not metal!) container. Add a pinch of salt.

2 Add 12-20 pennies. Let them stand for a few minutes while you do the next step.

3 Clean an iron nail with cleanser and rinse it with water.

4 Drop the nail into the vinegar and wait for 15 minutes.

5 When you drain off the vinegar, you'll find that two things have happened—the pennies are clean, and the iron nail is covered with a layer of copper.

What Happened

The acid in the vinegar removed the top layer of copper from the pennies, forming a compound called copper acetate.

The now-loose copper in the compound was attracted by the iron. It bonded to it, resulting in a coating of copper.

PHONY COIN FLIP

You can flip a coin and win nearly every time using this simple but exceptionally dishonest technique.

1 Use a quarter. The bigger your coin, the less likely you'll accidentally get an honest flip. Practice before you try using this in public.

2 Position the coin. Just like in an honest flip, curl your index finger around it and place your thumb under it. Glance down and notice which side is up—let's say it's "heads."

3 Work on the next moves to make sure

they don't look suspicious. Bring your hand down as in an honest flip. While your hand is moving, slip your thumb on top of the coin to steady it against your middle finger. Keep your index finger curled around it. Bend your wrist slightly.

4 As you throw your hand up to flip the coin, flick your wrist sideways, spinning the coin off the tip of your index finger . . . the way you might spin a tiny Frisbee.

5 Like a Frisbee toss, this sideways spin keeps the coin level on its flight upward, not letting it flip.

6 If your coin goes up "heads" it should come down "heads." If your friend calls "tails," let the coin land cleanly on your hand, taking care that you don't let it bounce. If your friend calls "heads," catch the coin and smoothly slap it onto the back of your wrist.

FUN WITH THE LAWS OF MOTION

Card Goes, Coin Stays

1 Balance a playing card on the tip of your finger.

2 Balance a quarter on top of the playing card.

3 Flick the edge of the card with a finger of your other hand.

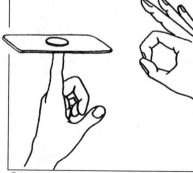

4 The playing card will sail away, leaving the quarter balanced neatly on your finger.

Coin on the Edge

1 Cut a long strip of paper. Put one end over the edge of a drinking glass.

2 Balance a quarter on the edge of the glass, on top of the paper.

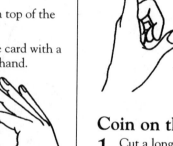

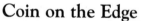

3 Simply pulling will usually dislodge the quarter. Instead, hold the paper with one hand and give a karate chop to the strip of paper with the other.

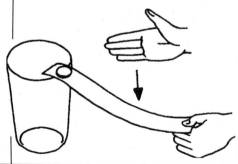

SPIT NICKELS

This requires a dozen nickels in your pocket and one clean enough to put in your mouth. Use this in any situation that needs a little livening up.

1 Secretly tuck a nickel into your cheek. Leave it there for a while. It won't interfere with your talking. Hide another in your right hand.

2 After a while, furrow your brow and look worried. Screw your mouth up in a funny way. Somebody might ask what's wrong. Say: "I've got something in my mouth . . ."

3 Open your mouth and reveal the nickel on your tongue. Look puzzled as you pretend to spit the nickel into your hand. (In reality, tuck it back into your cheek and

show the one you had hidden in your palm.) "That's weird," you say, putting the nickel into your pocket. "I'm sorry. You were saying . . . ?"

4 Make it look like you're stashing the nickel, but actually retain it in your palm. Wait for the conversation to get going again, then do the whole thing over again. And again. And again.

5 Finish up by coughing up a bunch of nickels, as in the next trick.

Note: This trick can be done with anything you can hold undetected in your mouth. Some people have performed it with hard-boiled eggs!

COUGH UP SOME CHANGE

This one is a variation on spitting nickels. While talking to a friend, you start coughing dryly into your hand.

You apologize and explain: "I was in a coffee shop this morning, drinking coffee. The place was crowded. The waiter was coming with my change (*cough, cough*) and somebody bumped his arm and he dumped it all over the table.

"Now, what I didn't know—" you cough again, more insistently, "was that he apparently dropped a dime into my coffee cup (*cough, cough*) and it still had coffee in it. I took one last big gulp and swallowed it. I could feel it going down my throat, but by that time (*cough, cough*) it was too late.

"Since then (*cough*) I've had this cough . . . (*cough, cough*). It's terrible. I just keep waiting for some kind of change." At that you start coughing harder. "No change in this cough all day," you gasp as you double over.

Finally, you give an especially hard cough and a nickel suddenly flies out of your mouth. You cough again and five pennies fly out.

Your coughing stops immediately. You sigh contentedly and say, "Whew, a nickel and five pennies— that's the change I've been waiting for."

How You Do It

Curl your fingers around the coins in the hand you're coughing into. Keep the nickel separate in the crack between your pinky and ring finger. On the first big cough, release the nickel; on the next, release all the pennies.

PSYCHIC TRICKS

Seers and Suckers

Interest in psychic phenomena has opened the door to con artists—phony "channelers," mind-readers, spoon-benders, and even "psychic surgeons" who use hidden balloons filled with blood to give the illusion of cutting painlessly through skin.

The bad news is that the con artists have ripped off a lot of people for money and more. The good news is that they've given the world some mighty fine tricks.

All of the tricks on the following pages have been used successfully on credulous people. Let's hope your friends aren't gullible enough to fall

for them. But if they are, why not convince them of your Amazing

Powers? As the saying goes: Never give a seeker an honest break.

STOP YOUR PULSE

The fakirs of India know tricks that have amazed people for centuries. Here's one of their finest: you announce that you can stop your heart at will! You lie down, breathe deeply, and apparently lose consciousness. Your volunteer feels your pulse getting weaker and weaker . . . and then disappear completely. When your volunteer hits a count of five your pulse begins again.

How You Do It

1 Weave a tale about the mystics' ability to control the body with the mind, to the amazement of doctors and scientists. Tell about an old fakir (pronounced, by the way, fah-KEER) who taught you how to stop your heart and then restart it. Be earnest and convincing.

2 Ask for a volunteer to monitor your pulse. Say: "I will be in a deep trance; I don't want to be in danger of losing track of the time, so when you feel my heart stop, slowly and loudly count to five."

3 Your volunteer actually

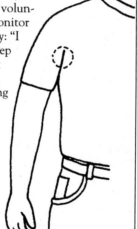

feels your pulse weaken and stop. After he or she counts to five, it starts again and you "wake up."

4 How do you do it? Easy. Before the trick, conceal a small rubber ball in your armpit. To stop your pulse, press your arm tightly against your body. The ball temporarily blocks the circulation in that arm, making it seem that your heart has stopped. For the short time of this trick (5-10 seconds) this is completely harmless—exactly what doctors do with that inflatable cuff when they check your blood pressure. (For safety, don't go beyond 5-10 seconds.)

5 After your friend has counted to five, relax your arm and your pulse will begin again.

LEVITATE A TABLE

The levitating table is a good effect by itself or in conjunction with the Phony Seance (see page 81). It has been used for at least a hundred years in seances and spirit communications.

1 The lighter the table, the easier it is to levitate it, of course. Make sure you wear shoes or boots with a good solid edge sticking out from the sole. And wear loose long sleeves so people don't see your muscles flexing.

2 Have four people sit around a card table. Dim the lights and speak in a soft voice. Ask them to press their hands on the table at the corners, palms down. Suggest that everybody touch their outer fingers together to assure that there is no trickery (this, of course, is complete misdirection).

3 Tell them about the mysterious psychic energy vortex that creates telekinetic energy in the spot where you're sitting, etc. Be convincing, then "go into a trance."

4 Press your hands firmly on the table and discreetly push to one side. The other side will slowly lift off the ground. Keep expressionless, and make sure your hands and arms reveal no effort.

5 Pull toward yourself next. The far end will go up. Push toward the right and the left side will go up. Lift your knee up and your end will go up. Make different sides go up randomly.

6 Now comes the climax of the whole trick. For your final tilt, make the right side go up. As the

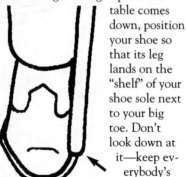

table comes down, position your shoe so that its leg lands on the "shelf" of your shoe sole next to your big toe. Don't look down at it—keep everybody's

attention above table level.

7 Make sure your right hand is positioned directly above the same table leg. Press straight down, *hard*, with your right hand. You are trying to clamp the table between your foot and hand.

8 Keeping your heel on the floor for leverage, lift your toes off the ground. This will cause the entire table to rise *straight up*, all four legs off the ground. Use your hand to steady the table and get all four legs off the ground for a second or two.

9 Don't worry if you can't hold it for very long. In fact, if the table slips off your shoe and crashes to the ground, it creates an even more dramatic impression than a slow, controlled descent.

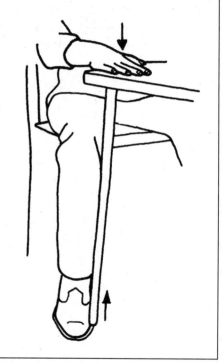

PHONY SEANCE

The best thing about seances is that everything takes place in the dark. There's a reason, as you'll see when you set up your own visitation by the spirits.

What You'll Need

- Table
- Cigarette lighter
- Candle
- 2 pieces of cardboard
- Pen
- 2 rubber bands
- Ambient music (optional)

How You Do It

1 Get everything ready. Black out windows and even door cracks— your room must be made completely dark. Put the lighter in your shirt pocket or right pants pocket.

2 Have your friends sit around the table, lit candle in center. Say:

"We are here tonight in a circle to see if the spirits are among us and whether they will communicate to us from the Other Side."

3 Show that the sides of both sheets of cardboard are blank. Wrap rubber bands around each end and put the package on the table with the pen on top of it. Say: "This is in case anybody from the Other Side wants to send us a message."

4 Have everyone place their hands palms down on the table. As you talk for a few moments about the spirits and the Other World, casually slide your hands to within a few inches of each other.

Take your right hand from your neighbor's wrist and reach toward the candle. In the movement of leaning forward, you'll casually pull your left hand toward the center. Snuff the flame with your fingers, and lean back in the darkness.

7 Here comes the trick: pull your left hand over and use it—*not* your right—to grip your neighbor's wrist. Now, unbeknownst to either of your neighbors, you have your right hand free.

8 Encourage everyone to concentrate on the spirits. As you talk about how to feel the presence of spirits, etc. (this is to mask any

sounds you make), feel around gently for the pen. Write "I AM WITH YOU" in ghostly letters on the cardboard. Turn the package over so the writing is on the bottom.

5 Tell everyone to reach over with their right hand and grasp the left wrist of the person to their right. Say: "This makes sure that nobody can pull any funny business."

6 You announce that you are now going to extinguish the candle.

9 After a short, meditative silence, say "We have been in the dark long enough; let us see if there has been a message. I shall light the candle." This gives you a reason to take your "right" hand from your neighbor's wrist.

10 Actually, you slip your *left* hand off your neighbor's wrist. Use your right hand to find your lighter and light the candle, using the movement of leaning forward to slide your left hand back toward your left neighbor.

11 Take both hands and take the rubber bands from the cardboard without showing the writing on the bottom. Lift the top piece and show it. Say, with a sigh of resignation and subtle reproach:

"Apparently we didn't have our energies fully focused on reaching the spirits. Let's try again."

12 Lift the piece of cardboard with writing on the bottom and slide the blank piece underneath, so the writing is inside. Put the rubber bands back around.

13 Say: "I think we need more direct psychic energy. Let us all lay our hands directly on

the piece of cardboard."

14 Snuff the candle again. Tell everyone to focus all their energies on receiving a message from the Other World. After a short while, say: "I think that is long enough." Light the candle again.

15 Ask: "Will somebody please open the package again to see if we received a message?"

16 Keep a blank face when people gasp at the sight of I AM WITH YOU. Explain nothing.

Getting in the Spirit

You can do a lot with that free right hand, like creating noisy spirit manifestations, moving things around the table, and waving white silks over the table for ghostly images.

BEND A SPOON

Some "psychics" are so blatant, it's amazing that people can take them seriously. One of the most famous, when walking with followers, would flip things high into the air from behind his back and then claim that the objects had "manifested themselves" from thin air. His followers believed him!

His best-known trick: He'd take a spoon and hold it lightly, stroking it with his finger. As he sweated with intensity, witnesses swore that the spoon slowly bent itself into a weird angle.

How You Do It

1 Pick up an expendable spoon and show that it is unbent.

2 While you lecture about Powers of the Mind, hold the spoon casually in your hand. Discreetly push your thumb *hard* against the bowl (left). If your grip is reasonably strong, most spoons will bend easily.

3 Grip the handle loosely to hide the fact that you've already bent

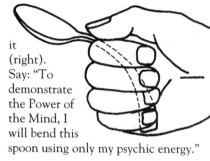

it (right). Say: "To demonstrate the Power of the Mind, I will bend this spoon using only my psychic energy."

4 Look intense. Rub the spoon lightly with your forefinger. After a period of vein-popping concentration, begin slow-w-w-ly advancing the handle of the spoon forward with your thumb, a millimeter at a time. It'll look like the handle is slowly bending before your friends' eyes.

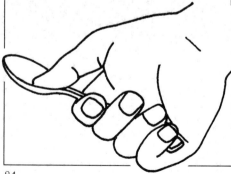

MORBID TRICKS

Dismember Me?

Jokes involving mock injuries and amputations are very popular with grade school kids . . . and with those who never grew out of that stage, like that uncle who played "I've got your nose" every time you saw him.

Psychologists tell us that these jokes are actually an attempt to deal safely with genuine distress—that they become "funny" at an age when kids are becoming conscious of their own vulnerability to the horrors that the jokes simulate.

We don't know about that. But from our comprehensive tests, we do know that these tricks will elicit a wide range of reactions, from "Cool!" to "Yech!" and "That's not funny!"

The reaction you get will depend in large part on how plausible your story is. Less can be more.

For example, when test marketing Break Your Nose, we found most

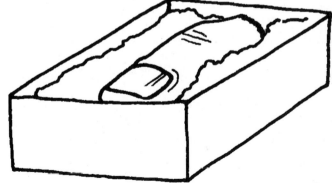

people, regardless of age, didn't react appreciably when we told them we were *breaking* our noses. They figured that it was just a trick, reasoning that not even *we* would purposely break our own noses. But when we did the trick after telling them that it felt good to crack our "nose joints," many were satisfyingly horrified and repulsed.

So for the best reaction, keep your story at least semi-plausible.

PULL OFF YOUR THUMB

1 Practice this with yourself in a mirror before trying it on people. Close your right hand and put its thumb between the index and middle fingers. Extend it over your middle finger as far as you can.

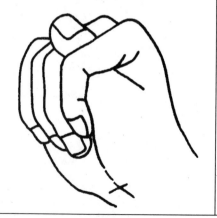

2 Close your left hand and bend its thumb as tightly as you can over its index finger.

3 Position your two hands together so that your right thumb looks as if it were really your left thumb. Slowly pull your hands apart while emoting severe pain and suffering.

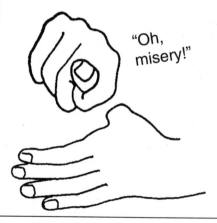

"Oh, misery!"

BREAK YOUR NOSE

As you bend your nose back and forth, bystanders will wince at the excruciating snapping sounds.

Snap!
Crackle!
Pop!

How You Do It

1 Say you're going to break your nose. Or, better yet, talk about how good it feels to sometimes crack your back or knuckles, but that you've never had an experience as profound as cracking the joints in your nose (technically, the nose has no joints, but no matter).

2 Hold your hands in the classic church bulletin prayer position (fingertips and palms together), with a hand on either side of your nose. Your thumbnails should be exactly at lip level, because you need to be able to sneak them to your mouth.

3 Push and pull with your hands, flexing your nose this way and that. If you hold just the tip but move your hands to the far left and right, you give the right impression.

4 Meanwhile, make the cracking noises by hooking your thumbnail behind a front tooth and snapping—like plucking a guitar string—each time you flex your nose. Combined with the visual effect, grown men will weep and women will faint. Or vice versa.

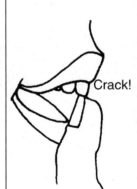

Crack!

MUMMIFIED FINGER

If you want to be a little morbid, tell your friends that it's from an Egyptian mummy. If you want to be *really* morbid, tell them you found it lying down by the railroad tracks. Whichever explanation you use, the Finger in the Box is a classically great trick.

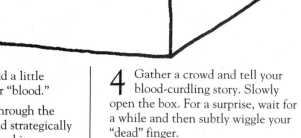

1 Find a small box and cut a hole in the side just big enough for your middle finger to poke through. Line it tastefully with cotton.

2 Rub your middle finger with flour or baby powder to make it look lifeless. If you'd like, add a little ketchup or red paint for "blood."

3 Poke your finger through the hole in the box and strategically arrange the cotton around it.

4 Gather a crowd and tell your blood-curdling story. Slowly open the box. For a surprise, wait for a while and then subtly wiggle your "dead" finger.

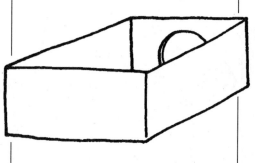

HAT TRICKS

A Real Show-Topper

It's too bad that people don't wear hats much anymore. Hats make a good prop for these tricks, most of which were developed during the hat-happy vaudeville era. Still, these stunts are pretty cool and may be worth finding a hat for.

Remember that a fragile hat will get pretty beat up, so try to find a strong felt one without cardboard supports. Heavier hats work better for tosses and flips than light ones.

Hats for either gender that are pro-portioned like a derby or top hat are good—floppier hats make it harder to do flips because of the added air resistance.

FLIP A HAT DOWN YOUR ARM

Casually flipping your hat off your head and down your arm into your outstretched hand makes a great impression as you enter a room.

1 Reach your right hand out, palm up, to the side and front. Your arm should be slightly downhill and nearly straight as if you're about to do the "Alas, poor Yorick . . ." scene from *Hamlet*.

2 As you look down your outstretched arm, reach up behind your head with your left hand and tap the hat with your index finger, aiming it down your arm.

3 Try it a few times just to get the feel of it. You're trying to flick it just hard enough that it tumbles end over end once and lands right side up in your hand.

4 There are four key benchmarks to see if you're getting it right. First, the front brim should touch your shoulder as it lands.

5 Next, the crown's first edge will touch at the top of your elbow joint. Then, the crown's trailing edge will hit just above your wrist.

6 Finally, the back of the brim should end up right at your hand, ready for you to catch it.

TOSS A HAT ONTO YOUR HEAD

This takes some practice, but not that much. And, if you've got a hat and the will to use it, the trick is worth the effort.

1 Whenever you have a spare moment, practice throwing your hat up into the air and catching it on a single flip. Hold it by the brim right side up, flip it a few feet into the air with a wrist-spin toward you, and catch it by the brim right side up after a single flip.

2 Get to the point where the hat will land predictably in your hand after a single rotation. At that point, try the same flip but duck your head instead of your hand under the hat.

3 The first dozen times, consider yourself lucky if it actually comes close to your head. Keep at it.

4 There are two steps you're working toward: getting the hat on your head, and getting it there without having to duck your head. Eventually, you'll be able to do it most of the time while maintaining the quiet dignity that comes from wearing a really nice hat.

COATRACK TOSS

Ever see anybody toss a hat and have it land on a hat rack, a hook on a wall—or even somebody else's head? Here's how to do it.

1 Hold out your hand, palm up, and place your hat right side up on it so your thumb is holding the brim and your fingers are inside the hat.

2 Bend your elbow and bring your arm up so that the hat is next to your ear, facing the target, about 4-5 feet away.

3 Toss the hat hard, directly at your target. You're doing it right if it makes one complete flip before landing perfectly.

OTHER HAT STUNTS

Nose Balance

It's easy to balance your hat on its brim on your hand. It's not too much harder to balance it on your foot or nose . . . with a little practice. The secret is to always watch the uppermost part of the brim.

If you're balancing on your nose, you can't see the uppermost part of the brim. No matter. Watch the center of the sweatband inside the hat. When you tilt your head forward it will fall right onto your head.

Two-Hand Dismount

1 Reach up with both hands, palms up, elbows upward and out. Grasp the hat with your fingers beneath the brim.

2 Lift the hat forward and rotate your wrists, tumbling the hat smoothly in your hands.

3 Continue rolling the hat as you lower it by turning the brim over your fingers like a baton, ending with it at stomach level, face up (this is an especially great move if you're a professional panhandler).

4 To put the hat back on, reverse the entire movement.

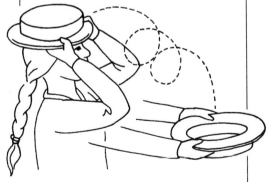

DOLLAR-BILL TRICKS

Paperclip Link

The power of money? Here's an easy trick that shows the magic of the Almighty Dollar. Although the props are modest, the effect is pretty mind-boggling: two paperclips fly into the air and link together before your very eyes.

1 Fold any denomination bill into a flattened **S** shape. (Using a five gives you a wonderfully awful punch line. Read on.)

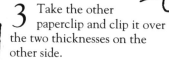

2 Take a paperclip and clip it over the two thicknesses at the end of the bill closest to you (see illustration).

3 Take the other paperclip and clip it over the two thicknesses on the other side.

4 Grab each end of the bill. Pull your hands away from each other, straightening the bill.

5 The two clips will fly into the air—and in the process, they'll have linked themselves together.

Awful punchline, if you use a $5 bill: "Why do the paperclips come together? That's because of the guy on the bill: it's Abraham . . . *Linkin'*."

Variation: If you also loop a rubber band around the bill, the paperclips will again end up linked . . . and hanging from the bill by the rubber band.

STRONG DOLLAR

I s a dollar strong enough to hold up a water glass without the support of the International Monetary Fund?

What You'll Need
- A crisp, new dollar bill
- 3 water glasses

How You Do It

1 Place two glasses about 4" apart and challenge onlookers to place a dollar bill across them in a way that it will support a third glass.

2 After they pronounce it impossible, take the dollar and fold it lengthwise in tiny accordion folds.

3 Place it across the two glasses. It should now support the weight of your third glass.

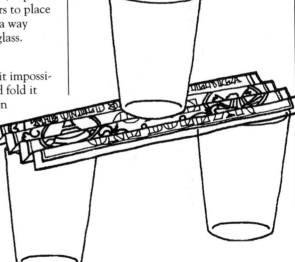

STUPID MONEY TRICKS

Breaking Bread

Hold a bread stick between your hands and challenge your tablemates to break it with a dollar bill folded in half. They can hack at it repeatedly and nothing will happen.

When it's your turn, sneak your index finger into the fold. The bread stick will break cleanly.

Double Your Money

Ask a spectator for a dollar bill. Say: "I can show you how to double your money."

Fold the dollar solidly in half. Say: "I've doubled your money. Look— you can see it *in creases*."

Turn a One into a Five

If the last trick doesn't satisfy, say that you can guarantee that you can turn a one dollar bill into a five.

Take the dollar bill, roll it up lengthwise into a rope, and bend it into the numeral **5**.

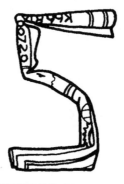

Uncatchable Dollar

If you can catch it you can keep it. That's the challenge you give when you pull out a dollar bill.

To demonstrate, you dangle a bill with your right hand. With your left hand, you hold your thumb and forefinger one inch apart at George Washington's head. When you let go with the right hand, you easily catch it with your left.

It looks simple. But it isn't. Have another person try to catch it from that position. They'll find it's virtually impossible. They don't have enough time to react before the dollar slips away . . . sort of a metaphor for real life.

PLATE SPINNING

Take It for a Spin

Plate spinning is an impressive trick. Yet, the basics aren't that hard to learn.

After a little preparation and just a few hours of practice—and a few broken plates—you can be delighting crowds with one good turn after another.

What You'll Need

• **Plates.** Look for expendable china at resale stores or garage sales. Each must have a well-defined circular lip around its bottom and a shallow indentation in the exact center of the bottom (otherwise drill one using a $1/4$" bit).

• **Stick.** A dowel about 3 feet long and $1/4$ inch in diameter. Use a pocket knife to taper one end of your stick into a rounded point.

• **Soft grass.** Stay away from pets, kids, cars, tree roots, and sidewalks. The plates are fragile, yet also heavy. If one falls on something or somebody, it can break or do damage.

BASIC SPIN

You need to learn the basic spin before you can go on to other stunts. But it's also a good trick in and of itself.

How You Do It

1 Hold your stick up so its point is at chest level. Center your plate on top of it with the stick's point nestled into the center hollow you found or drilled.

2 Grasping the plate's rim with your free hand, spin the plate toward yourself (see left). If it falls, try again. With a few dozen tries you should be able to get the plate to spin on the stick.

3 With the flat of your free hand, stroke the rim of the plate in the direction of its spin to speed it up. Stroke it gently but firmly and you won't dislodge it from the stick.

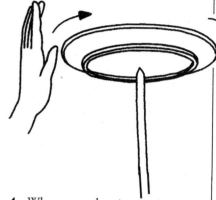

4 When your plate is spinning steadily, lift your stick and hold it triumphantly up and away from your body. The plate will spin there for a surprisingly long time.

5 When your plate starts to wobble, you can stop it with your hand or repeat steps 3 and 4.

RIM TWIRLING

In the last trick, you had to keep the plate spinning by stroking it with your hand. But there's a way to control the plate's spin with your stick by twirling the stick against the inside ridge of the plate.

This is easier than it sounds, because a spinning plate has a great deal of gyroscopic stability. It may take a couple of attempts before you get it. If you don't get discouraged and don't let the falling plate land on your head or foot, you'll get it.

How You Do It

1 Spin an invisible plate. Steady your stick with your index finger, point it straight up in the air, and draw 6" circles in the sky. Visualize a plate at the end of your stick. When this movement feels natural, go on to the next step.

2 Do the Basic Spin and speed it up with your hand. As the plate hums merrily along, move your hand down to the end of your stick, index finger up, and remember how it felt to draw circles in the sky. In a second you're going to do the same thing with a real plate.

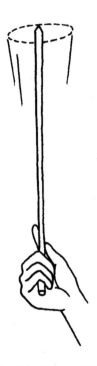

4 The stick will quickly slide toward the rim of the plate . . . and, if you're not prepared, right off the edge. Before that can happen, start drawing sky circles. After a few wobbles, you'll catch the rim, get into the rhythm of the plate's spin, and amaze yourself!

5 You'll notice that you can affect the speed of the plate's spin. Try spinning your plate as fast as you can. Then see how slowly you can go before you get a dangerous-looking wobble. Find a speed that provides a stable spin with as little effort as possible.

6 To stop, simply let go of your stick and let it fall. The plate will fall straight down, still spinning. Step back and catch it with both hands, as if it were a Frisbee.

3 Lift your stick high. Try to jar the point of it out of the indentation by giving the stick a light nudge, lift, or push.

ADVANCED PLATE TRICKS

When you have the basics down, you can start working on some additional variations.

Balances

If you can balance a broomstick on your palm, foot, forehead, or chin (see page 119), you can do the same with a plate spinning on a stick.

Flying Saucers

When you've got a good spin going, give your stick a light jerk upward so that your plate spins smoothly into the air like a Frisbee. When it comes back down, catch it on the end of your stick by lowering your stick hand quickly. This allows a soft landing—otherwise, the plate will bounce off.

Full Setting

• Have a friend spin plates and hand the sticks to you one at a time. How many can you twirl at once?

• Stick any number of pointy sticks into the ground. Spin a plate on each. Stay awake and refresh each plate's spin when it starts wobbling. Frantic fun!

BUILD AN IGLOO

Give Up Snow Business?

Building a real igloo was an unrealized goal on snow days when we were kids in the Midwest. The problem was we didn't know what we were doing: getting that round shape without having the roof cave in was beyond our skills.

That's why we were glad to run across an account of igloo building by native Canadians, in a book called *The Igloo* by David and Charlotte Yue (Houghton-Mifflin, 1988).

Background

• *Iglu* is a native word meaning any kind of house.

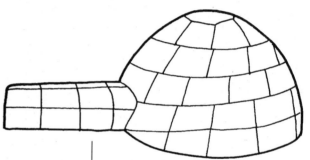

• Igloos were traditionally used in Central Canada for about half the year, from October until spring.

• Not all native groups in the Arctic used igloos; some never used them, while others used them only as temporary shelter while traveling.

• A good builder can build a basic igloo model in a little over an hour.

• Snow is a great insulator: the average temperature inside an igloo is 65° warmer than the outside. The dome structure is energy efficient, allowing the most space with the least amount of surface area.

• The domes are also very strong, allowing native kids to slide down them for fun.

What You'll Need

• A 3'-deep drift of packed snow as big as your intended igloo. (If necessary, create one by piling snow and letting it sit overnight.)

• A large kitchen knife. A curved blade made of caribou antler is traditional, but few homes stock them any more. If kids are involved, keep them away from the knife and responsible adult who is doing the cutting. (We haven't tried a metal ruler, but it might work where safety is a special concern.)

How You Do It

1 Draw a circle in the snow as a guideline. For sleeping 4 or 5 people, figure about 9'-12' in diameter and 7'-9' high.

2 Draw the entrance passageway —two parallel lines about 30"-40" apart and about 6' long. If you are on a slope, point the passage downhill (this'll keep heat from leaking out).

3 Cut 1-2 feet deep into your two parallel lines. Remove and discard a wedge-shaped block from the end to give your igloo a

ramped entrance and allow you room when cutting blocks.

4 Start cutting building blocks from between your two cuts. Cut them 1'-2' deep, 4"-6" thick, and as wide as your passageway. Don't cut them straight—make them "curving rectangles," corresponding to the circle shape of the igloo. Keep cutting blocks of the same size and shape as you dig up to and then through the circle you've drawn.

5 When you've accumulated a dozen blocks and have cut away some working room inside the circle, jam one of the blocks back into the trough exactly where the wall of the igloo will go (see below).

6 Next arrange your blocks in a layer around your circle, shaving a wedge off the bottom and sides of each so it leans inward. Each block will support the others so that your walls will always stay in place without additional props.

7 Before you add the next layer of blocks, take your knife and cut two standing blocks in a diagonal from the far lower corner of one to the far upper corner of the other (see right).

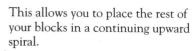

This allows you to place the rest of your blocks in a continuing upward spiral.

8 From here on, you work from the inside of the igloo, cutting blocks out from the "floor," shaping them, and positioning them on the spiral. After you place a block, carefully run your knife up and down along where it touches the other blocks. This softens the snow and smooths out irregularities, allowing for an airtight fit.

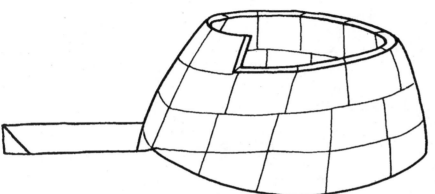

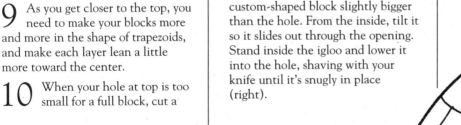

9 As you get closer to the top, you need to make your blocks more and more in the shape of trapezoids, and make each layer lean a little more toward the center.

10 When your hole at top is too small for a full block, cut a custom-shaped block slightly bigger than the hole. From the inside, tilt it so it slides out through the opening. Stand inside the igloo and lower it into the hole, shaving with your knife until it's snugly in place (right).

11 You're now inside a fully enclosed dome. There shouldn't be any holes in the walls or ceiling—if you see any, jam a little soft snow into the cracks.

12 For ventilation and light, cut a small hole (about 6" in diameter) into the top. If windy, put it slightly off-center away from the wind.

13 Find the block you put in the passageway and cut a door big enough to crawl through.

14 Begin cutting blocks for your enclosed passageway with an eye to preserving ledge space for sitting, lounging, and working on. Shape them so they curve and lean inward, and place them over your passageway. Save a big block for a door.

15 A candle or small lamp inside will give you light, and it will also melt a thin inside layer of snow, which is good: the melted snow freezes up again, sealing the igloo walls and making it even warmer.

16 **IMPORTANT SAFETY WARNING:** *If you use a lamp, make sure that you have an adequate vent hole on top. And* **never** *light a fire or heater inside your igloo, even with a vent hole, because you could suffocate.*

17 If the igloo gets too stuffy, enlarge the vent hole up to 6"-8". If it gets too cold, stuff a rag or mitten loosely into it (don't seal it completely, though, because you want *some* ventilation).

18 When your igloo melts away, don't feel bad. In the Arctic, an igloo is used only for a month or so before being abandoned.

MUSICAL TRICKS

Music Hath Charms

As far as we can guess, music was among the earliest discoveries of humanity. Before the wheel, before fire, people figured out that they could create sounds that were pleasing to the ear and mind.

Early music was heavy on voice and percussion. Strings and reeds eventually emerged, followed later by brasses, then eventually by electric guitars and electronic synthesizers and samplers.

But let's go back to those simpler days when music was homemade from whatever was on hand. Who knows? We might start a trend. Maybe even discover the Next Big Thing.

WATER-GLASS GLOCKENSPIEL

Fill Up Glass?

One of the great lost novelty acts, last seen on TV around 1958, was the guy who played music on water glasses. You don't see that on MTV now, for some reason. Too bad, because there's a great "Fill Up Glass" pun forever waiting unborn.

How You Do It

1 Line up 4-5 large glasses and 3-4 medium or small ones. Start with the large glasses. Fill one to the top with water. Tap it with a spoon. When you sing DO-RE-MI, that'll be low DO.

2 Fill the next large glass less full. Sing DO-RE . . . and tap the glass. Add or pour out water until it sounds like RE. More water makes the tone lower; less water, higher.

3 Go through MI, FA, SO, etc., adjusting the water each time. You'll have to switch to the smaller glasses on FA or SO.

4 Then, check your tuning. Play your first glass (low DO) and your last (high DO). They should be the same note, one octave apart. If you hear an "unng-unng-unng" vibrating sound, you're not quite there.

5 Play the entire scale—does it sound right? Tap DO, MI, SO, high DO in quick succession—do they sound pretty . . . or pretty bad? Keep tuning until it sounds "SO-FA, so good."

6 Try some simple songs. Use a spoon in each hand for speed. Play *Mary Had a Little Lamb*:

Mi Re Do Re Mi Mi Mi
Re Re Re Mi So So
Mi Re Do Re Mi Mi Mi Mi
Re Re Mi Re Do.

CRYSTAL RINGING

Rubbing your wetted finger lightly on the rim of a wineglass can create an ethereal tone that fills a room. In fact, Benjamin Franklin, inspired by this after-dinner activity, invented an instrument called a glass harmonica that consisted of spinning glass disks that were stroked with wet fingertips. Many composers wrote music specifically for it, most notably Mozart.

How You Do It

1 Get out some stemmed wineglasses or water glasses. It's a good sign if they make a sharp, ringing "ping" when you tap them with your fingernail.

2 Hold your glass by the stem. Dip your free index finger into water and lightly rub it around the top of your glass.

3 At first you may hear only disappointing little squeaks, or nothing, but keep at it. At some point, sooner or later, a clear tone will suddenly ring out.

4 Until you hear the sound, re-wet your finger every 10-15 seconds. After that, re-wet your finger only when your tone becomes parched.

5 The amount of liquid in the glass changes the pitch. You and your friends can get some beautiful chords (or ear-piercing ones) if you tune your glasses to different tones. For psychedelic effects, tilt or slosh the water as you play.

PLAY SPOONS

Playing the spoons is a great way to add percussion to any home-made or recorded music . . . or simply to work off your edgy urban nervous energy in a downhome manner.

How You Do It

1 Get yourself a couple of spoons and a rural attitude.

2 Let the fingers of your most co-ordinated hand go completely limp into a relaxed half-fist.

3 Take your first spoon and turn it *facedown*. Slide the handle between your index and middle fingers.

4 Take your second spoon and lay it *right side up* above the first

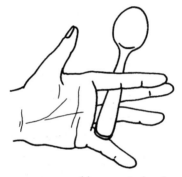

spoon, separated by your index finger. Hold it in place with your thumb. The two spoons should now be facing away from each other.

5 Adjust your grip so that the two spoon handles are nearly touch-

ing in back, and the back-to-back bowls are separated by about half an inch of air.

6 Diagnostic test time: Tighten your grip on the spoons. Wave them rhythmically in the air. You should hear no noise at all, because the spoons shouldn't touch yet. If the bowls are banging together, your grip is too loose. If the handles are rat-

tling, reposition your index finger to separate them more.

7 Sit down. Tighten your grip again. Using only a wrist movement, begin tapping the bottom spoon lightly against your thigh. If your grip is too tight, you may hear either nothing or a tinny little click.

8 Keep tapping and s-l-o-w-l-y begin relaxing your grip until you hear one rich, loud *bam!* each time you tap. If your spoons start slipping out of position, or if you hear little clicks between bams, you've loosened your hand too much.

9 Now let's make some music. Keep that basic rhythm going on your thigh, but bring your other hand into range and see what happens when you start tapping it on the upswing—the sound goes from *bum*

bum bum bum to *budda budda budda budda*. Move your hand in and out of spoon range and listen to the cool rhythms that develop: *bum budda budda bum bum budda bum*.

10 Play along with anything you can—country, rock, folk, hiphop, salsa, polkas, heavy metal, Bach . . . even political speeches (get with those Al Gore rhythms!).

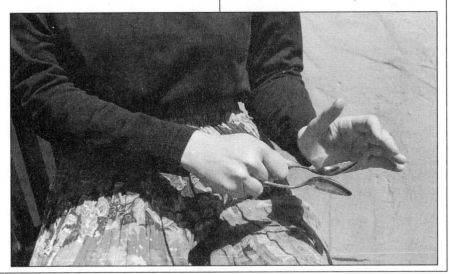

MUSICAL SAW

Join the Carpenters

When we say that you can join the Carpenters, we're not talking about the defunct musical group from the 1970s, but the *trade* group. Because we want to start you playing the musical saw.

Professional saw players usually cheat—they don't generally use truly functional saws. They also use violin bows. Being musical purists, we suggest that you use a rubber-handled screwdriver instead.

How You Do It

1 Use a standard wood saw with a flexible blade—the more flexible, the better.

2 Put the tip of the blade on a hard floor and stand on it with one foot (make sure you're wearing a shoe). Holding the handle in your hand, bend the saw into an elongated **S** shape.

3 Tap the saw blade with your rubberized screwdriver. Change the saw's tone by flexing the blade. To get that weepy vibrato, shake your hand slightly as you play.

HAND FLUTE

In South America, hand whistling has been used for centuries of musicmaking. A good hand whistler can create a melancholy flutelike sound that resembles nothing else.

The first note is the hardest. Once you get it, you can hit other notes just by opening one of your hands a little.

How You Do It

1 Cup your hands, sealing up all the cracks. Some people like to dip their hands in water first for a better seal.

2 Create an opening between your thumbs. You can test your seal now by pursing your lips around the opening and blowing in and out—if you can feel your hands being pushed and pulled by the air pressure, your seal is good.

3 Your thumbs should be bent slightly. Pucker your lips and put them on your thumbnails and knuckles (as indicated by the dotted oval on the next page).

4 Keep your lips puckered and blow. Don't puff your cheeks. You should feel the air rushing through the crack between your thumbs and *across the opening*. The idea is that half of the air should rush *across* the hole and half *into* it—like blowing across an empty Coke bottle that you've turned upside down.

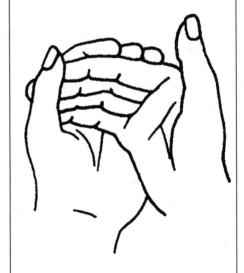

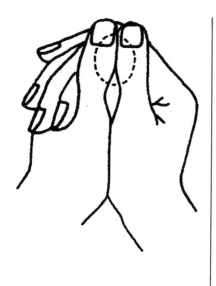

5 Hear something? Yeah, the sound of rushing wind, but no whistle. Okay, now's the time to troubleshoot. Are your lips puckered and not smashed against your knuckles?

6 Other ideas: Try tilting your hands down more. Try changing the size and shape of your opening. Try blowing harder . . . or softer. And check again to make sure your hands aren't leaking.

7 Are you thoroughly discouraged yet? Quit. Take a break. Don't even *think* about hand whistling for a while.

8 Later on, when you're stuck in traffic, waiting for a store to open or sitting through a long business meeting, try again. Once you get it, it'll all seem so simple.

9 When you can consistently get a clear, sweet tone, you're ready to start thinking about changing notes. Flutter your hands slightly.

10 Even a rank amateur like yourself can play an octave or more if you keep practicing. Who knows? You might get good enough to move to Bolivia, start a band, and glad-hand your way into the La Paz Philharmonic.

VENTRILOQUISM

Don't Read My Lips

Ventriloquism, from the Latin for "belly talk," has been traced as far back as early Greece and China, where it was used by priests to make the gods "talk." The famous Oracle of Delphi was believed to have been a ventriloquist's trick; the Greek philosopher Euricles made bird voices for entertaining guests.

During the Middle Ages, ventriloquism was equated with witchcraft, and practitioners were routinely burned at the stake.

Finally, in the 1700s, ventriloquism began catching on as entertainment. The art came to America at the dawn of the 19th century.

Finding Your Voice

To pull off the illlusion you need a voice that differs from your normal one. Most ventriloquists use a falsetto voice that comes simultaneously from both throat and nasal passages, which diffuses the sound so the listener can't pinpoint its origin. Here's an easy way to find your ideal dummy voice.

I suffer from mannequin depression

1 Push from the bottom of your lungs as you start saying the word "lean." Hold the "e" sound, feeling it buzz in your throat and nose, holding your tongue behind your bottom teeth.

2 Now start saying the word "cat" in the same voice but hold the "a" sound. Listen for that buzz.

3 Go to your mirror and watch your lips as you recite this modified alphabet in this new voice (difficult consonants have been temporarily removed):

**A C D E G H I J K L N O P
Q R S T U X Y Z**

4 Practice it until your lips don't move. Now you're ready to go on to harder sounds.

TALKING LIKE A DUMMY

The sounds you just practiced aren't too hard. But now you need to work on the difficult sounds—the ones that normally require lips. Here are substitutions professionals use.

W Say "oo-" and then the rest of the word. "We" is "oo-e"; "swell" is "soo-ell." Try this in front of the mirror: *We went with sweet Woodrow Wilson.*

F Widen your tongue and *say* "th" while you *think* "f." Emphasize the end of the word. For example, think "first" and say "thirst." Try this: *Father's fun enough on the phone.*

V Widen your tongue and *say* "th" while you *think* "v." So "vaguely" is said "they-glee" and "souvenir" becomes "soothe-an-ear." Try this: *Save a little veal for Valerie.*

M Say "nng" with a slight humming at the beginning and think "m." Try: *Mary had meringue and lamb* ("nng-a-rangg and la-nng-uh").

B B is tricky. Loosen and widen your tongue against the roof of your mouth and try to say a cross between "d" and a soft "th" (as in "thin") while thinking "b." Try this: *Bertha, bring me a bottle of beer.*

P P is tricky, too. Loosen your tongue, put it to the roof of your mouth and try a cross between "t," "d," and a soft "th," while thinking "p." Try this: *Porky Pig will gyp you.*

Instant Hand Puppet

Need a partner—fast? A pen and some lipstick is enough to transform your hand into a special friend. Add a hat, scarf, yarn wig, or doll clothes to complete the low-tech illusion.

WATCH YOUR MOUTH!

Practice is the key to being a convincing ventriloquist. Whether you buy a real dummy or make one with some lipstick and your hand, you'll have to be convincing enough that people will believe the illusion.

1 Work on talking with your new voice. In front of the mirror, watch for lip movement.

2 Practice when you can. If you can't look at a mirror (like when you're driving), put the fingers of one hand on your lips and see if you can feel any movement.

3 Want to look like a pro? Try a half-smile instead of a clenched jaw. Now and again look at your

dummy and react instead of staring vacantly.

4 If you want to improve fast, watch yourself on video.

Sing While Drinking

How does your dummy sing while you drink from a glass? Isn't that physiologically impossible? Yes, it is. Unless, of course, you know the trick.

1 During most of your dummy's song, simply *pretend* to drink.

2 At the song's last note, take a big swig but don't swallow. Keep the liquid in your mouth while continuing to hum the note.

3 End the song with a flourish. Have your dummy bow to take attention away from you, and at the same time pull out a handkerchief. As you wipe your mouth, *swallow*.

THROW YOUR VOICE

You can't really "throw" your voice—it always comes from inside your body. However, you can change frequencies and volume, bounce sound off a far wall, obscure where your voice is coming from, and create an amazing illusion.

Muffled Voice

Do you want to make it sound like somebody's locked in a trunk? Sounds from inside something lack high frequencies, which bounce off walls instead of penetrating them. Lock your tongue against the back of your top teeth, near the gum line. That'll bury your voice deep in the throat and make your consonants muffled.

Lower your volume. Turn toward the supposed sound source to divert attention from you, and also bounce

the sound from that direction. When you open the trunk or closet, go suddenly back to normal voice.

Telephone Voice

The key to the phone voice is to release as little air as possible. You almost have to hold your breath and squeeze out each word to simulate that electronic timbre. It can be tiring, so keep your conversations short at first.

The sound should come from the back of your mouth. Unlike the muffled voice, where you can turn your back to the audience, your ventriloquism has to be perfect, since everybody will be watching your mouth.

BALANCING TRICKS

Keeping It Up

Balancing stuff is not so hard. Anybody willing to practice can go from the simply amusing to the downright astounding in a fairly short time.

To learn, all you need is something to balance and some persistence. After all, you mastered the most difficult balancing stunt of all: standing on your own two feet. And at a tender age, yet!

Hand Balance

1 Balancing a tall object is much easier than balancing a short one. Find something at least 3-5 feet tall and not too heavy. Indoors, a peacock feather is good for beginners, because its wind resistance makes it move in slow motion, and it won't break anything when it falls. Or try a dowel, yardstick, broomstick, or cardboard tube.

2 Place the end of your pole on the flat of your palm.

3 Keep your eyes fixed on the *top* of your pole. You'll find your hand automatically adjusting to keep the pole from falling.

4 As you get the hang of it, try balancing the pole on your knuckles, your finger, your forearm, your knee, or your foot.

5 When you get *really* good, try using unexpected items like mops, light furniture, umbrellas, or even sticks topped with spinning plates (see page 97).

FACE BALANCE

Once you have the hand balance down, you're ready to try it on your chin, nose, or forehead. The easiest way is by incremental steps.

1 Do a hand balance at chest level, but try keeping your hand still: balance by moving your *body only*. Remember to keep your eye on the top of the pole.

2 Next, do a balance with your hand right next to your chin (if the palm position is too awkward, balance on your knuckles).

3 Next, try the pole on your chin. It'll take some time—your neck may get sore from bending backward. At first even a second of balancing may seem impossible, but keep working on it. Try your forehead next and then your nose.

4 If you ultimately want to balance pencils or silverware on your nose (and don't we all?), get a thin dowel about 36" long. When you can balance it easily, cut a 3" piece off. Do it again. Keep cutting and balancing until you get to about 10" long—the length of chopsticks, spoons, and pens.

DINNER-TABLE TRICKS

Waiting for your food to be served in a restaurant? Looking for a way to amuse yourself between courses at a family dinner?

These are tricks that will endear you to everyone at the table . . . except maybe the person who actually owns the fine crystal that you're trying to flip spoons into.

For a few of these tricks, you'll need extra props not normally found on the table, specifically string and toothpicks.

Remember to try these tricks at home first so you don't do damage or embarrass yourself in public.

Have fun! *Bon appetit!*

Wineglass Balance

This one looks downright scary, but it's mostly harmless. *Practice at home first.*

1 Hold a dinner plate on its edge with one hand. Your thumb is toward you on the bottom side of the plate, hidden from your companions.

2 Pick up a wineglass, preferably with a little liquid still in it, and hold it on the top edge of the plate. Subtly adjust it a few times, like you're trying to find the balance point. Get it "just right"—and let go. People will be amazed when the wineglass "balances" precariously on top.

3 What they don't know is that you're holding it up from behind with your thumb.

WRECKING THE SILVERWARE

Friends and Alloys

You bend a spoon into a **U** shape —and then restore it to its original form again.

How You Do It

1 Try this trick in front of the mirror a few times until it looks just right. Hide a dime in your right hand between your thumb and the first joint of your index finger.

2 Pick up a teaspoon admiringly and ask "What kind of metal is this?" Regardless of the answer, you say, "Hm, it looks like that new ultraflexible alloy."

3 Stand the spoon with its bowl on the table. Bring your right hand up to grasp its handle between your ring finger and pinky.

4 Position the tip of the handle to where you've hidden the dime. Reveal just a sliver of the dime. People will assume they're seeing the tip of the spoon's handle.

5 Cover your right hand with your left so that only the dime and the bowl of the spoon show. Push down and let the

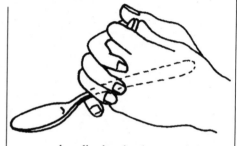

spoon handle slip slowly toward the base of your right thumb. Flex it a few times. With the dime in position, it looks like the spoon has turned to rubber.

6 Say: "Don't worry, it springs right back." Drop the spoon onto the table—Amazing! It's now restored!—and palm the coin.

GLASS SUSPENSION

Support the Middle Glass

This is a trick that will make everybody nervous: four knives supporting a glass in the air, balanced on top of four other glasses.

1 Arrange five glasses as shown. The middle one is just there temporarily to get the knives positioned.

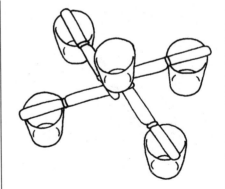

2 Next, wedge the knives securely together, as shown in the drawing above.

3 Carefully remove the middle glass. If the knives don't fall to the table with a scary clatter, you've done it right. Center the glass gently on top of the square where the knife blades intersect. *Voila!*

BOTTLE SUSPENSION

The bottle seems to defy gravity as it hangs from a thread on the handle of a table knife.

This is a trick that is partly optical illusion, but mostly a matter of manipulating the bottle's center of gravity to make it *look* like you're accomplishing the impossible.

You'll need a bottle, a table knife, and a short string.

1 Wait until a wine bottle is about $1/3$ full, or take an empty bottle and fill it $1/3$ full with water.

2 Cork the bottle and tie the string around its neck. Make sure it is tied tightly so the bottle can't slip out.

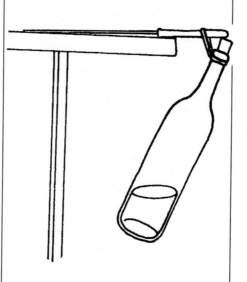

3 Tie the two loose ends of the string together to make another loop. This loop should be fairly small. You'll see why in a second.

4 Put the knife on the table with its handle hanging over the edge. Slip the loop over the end of the knife handle. The loop has to be small enough that your bottle is forced into slanting toward the table.

5 Don't let go yet. Adjust the bottle and knife carefully. When you get it right, you can pull your hand away. The bottle will swing alarmingly—but harmlessly—from the handle of the knife, apparently defying all known laws of gravity.

TIDDLY SPOONS

Let's Do Launch

You can use one spoon to flip another off the table and into a glass. Do it just for fun, or keep score and have a Souper Bowl.

1 Clear off breakables, set up a sturdy cup or glass to aim for, and make sure each player has two spoons. Agree to ground rules and scoring: How about 20 tries, five points for a solid landing, and one for bouncing off the top?

2 Set a spoon close to the glass with handle pointing toward it. This is the cannonball. Put another spoon in the same alignment, with handle under the first spoon's bowl. This is the launcher.

3 Hit the tip of the launcher's bowl with your closed fist. If you've lined up the spoons correctly, hit the launcher with the right amount of force, and allowed for wind patterns and magnetic fields, the cannonball spoon will flip clangingly into the glass.

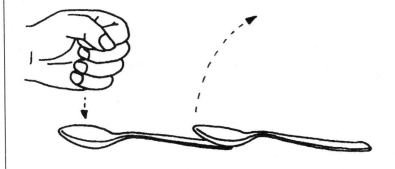

FLYING SAUCER

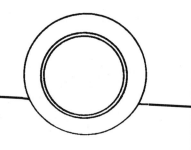

This is another stunt involving skill, dexterity, and jeopardy to place settings. We suggest trying it on a soft couch first.

1 Place a saucer upside down with its lip extending beyond the edge of the table (or couch).

2 Point your index finger under the overhanging lip of the saucer.

3 What you propose to do is flip the saucer into the air with your finger and catch it between your thumb and middle finger before it lands again on the table (or couch).

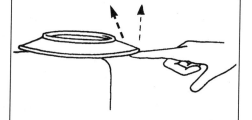

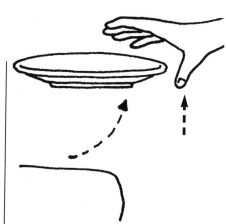

4 It's not actually that hard. The far edge of the saucer will virtually roll into your grip on your upward stroke.

KNIFE IN THE DINNER ROLL

You casually pull off a small piece of your dinner roll and eat it. "Pass the butter, please?" you ask.

When the butter arrives, you look confused. "Excuse me, has anybody seen my knife? Wait a minute—what the heck is this? Never mind!" You dig at the crust with your fingers, and slowly pull a knife out of the center of the roll. Seemingly oblivious to the chaos you've created, you happily butter your roll.

How You Do It

1 Secretly slip a butter knife under your watchband inside your wrist. The tip of the knife should rest just below your middle finger.

2 Rest your arm on the table, turning your body to conceal the knife from your companions.

3 Poke a hole in the bottom of your roll with your finger and pinch a bit of bread from the top of the roll. Poke the knife through the bottom hole until it's nearly sticking out of the top one.

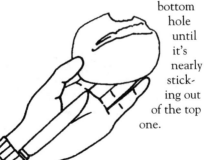

4 You're ready to begin. Ask for the butter, look confused, and do the shtick above.

5 When all eyes are on you, "discover" your knife in your roll. Slowly pull it out, and turn your attention to buttering.

Variations: You can pull almost anything long and thin out of your roll like a pen to sign the check or a bread stick ("Look, the miracle of birth!").

LEVITATING SALT SHAKER

There is no time like mealtime for revealing your hidden powers of levitation. Here are two demonstrations of your awesome abilities. Please use these secrets only for good—not for evil.

Assault on Gravity

1 Hide a toothpick behind your middle finger and secretly hold it there with your thumb.

2 Put a salt shaker in front of you. Announce that the secrets of levitation have been taught you by your esteemed guru, A. Baba Reba.

3 Stand up. Continue talking about how Baba Reba taught you that the laws of gravity can be disregarded if you have a good cosmic lawyer, etc.

4 Place your middle finger on the top of the salt shaker. Craftily wedge your hidden toothpick into one of the shaker's holes.

5 Command the salt shaker to rise. Lift your arm and levitate the shaker a few inches off the table. Point your mid-

dle and index fingers and curl the others.

6 Slowly bring the shaker back to earth and dislodge the toothpick. Take your hand away.

7 Announce: *"You have just witnessed a miracle!"* Hide the toothpick in your lap; don't repeat the trick.

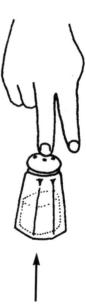

Levitating Bread Stick

This is a good follow-up to the last trick. It's an old trick; but if somebody claims to know it there's even a variation to confound them.

1 Hold a breadstick (or a knife or chopstick) in your left fist. Turn your hand toward you and away from your companions.

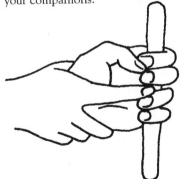

2 Grasp your wrist with your right hand. Sneak your right index finger up into your hand and rest it on the breadstick to hold it in place.

3 Announce that the great Baba Reba has not only taught you the powers of antigravity but of personal magnetism as well. With great concentration, slowly open your fist—the breadstick stays attached to your hand!

4 That's the trick. But since this is an old one, somebody may say they can do it, too. If so, challenge them to demonstrate.

5 As they do, secretly slip a knife under your watchband as in Knife in the Dinner Roll (page 127).

6 Do the trick again, doing the same routine as before. But *this* time, wedge the breadstick under the

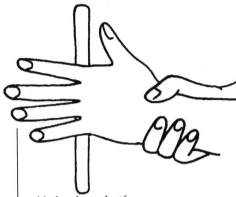

blade of your knife.

7 Say: "One thing Baba Reba taught me was to never take the other hand away." With that, you pull your right hand away from your wrist. The breadstick stays in place.

8 Hand the breadstick back to your challenger with your right hand, suggesting he or she try it your way. Meanwhile, slide your left into your lap and hide the knife.

SALT BECOMES PEPPER

Changing Seasons

You take a clear glass shaker, very obviously full of salt, and when you pour it, pepper comes out. You can present it as a magic trick ("I'm going to change this salt into pepper, and that's nothing to sneeze at!") or just use it for promoting general chaos and befuddlement.

How You Do It

1 Unscrew the cover of a clear glass salt shaker with salt in it.

2 Lay a paper napkin over the top. Push the napkin into the shaker, creating a shallow pocket.

3 Fill this pocket with pepper. Screw the cover back onto the shaker, being careful not to tear the napkin inside. If you don't see flecks of pepper falling into the salt, you're okay.

4 Carefully tear away the excess paper from the napkin that's sticking out from around the edge of the cover.

5 Now, when someone shakes the salt, pepper will come out. (You can, of course, make the reverse happen as well.)

BOUNCING APPLES

While seated at a table, you take an apple and suddenly toss it to the floor. It bounces back up, nearly to the ceiling. You catch it and nonchalantly return it to the table. Next you do the same with a pear, a roll, a hard-boiled egg . . .

How You Do It

1 Begin by distractedly inspecting pieces of fruit: hefting, shaking, putting them back. If anybody asks about it, give a vague reply like "It has to be just ripe enough . . ."

2 Finally you pick one. Suddenly, lift it above shoulder level and pitch it toward the floor, as hard as you can.

3 Actually, you don't let go. Nobody can see that, though, because your hand is below table level.

4 At *exactly* the same time, tap your foot against the floor. Don't wait—despite all logic, the illusion works best if you tap as soon as your arm goes down.

5 On the "rebound," flip the apple straight into the air with your wrist and fingers, making sure that your upper arm, in sight above table level, stays still.

6 Catch the apple when it comes down.

Note: When performed properly, the trick looks pretty amazing.

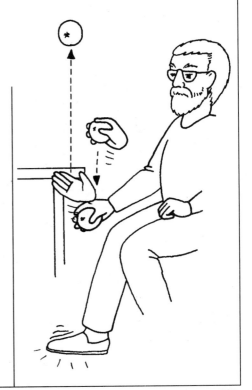

TABLECLOTH JERK

What's the classic stunt that is famous for never working right—with disastrous results? The old jerk-the-tablecloth bit. We don't recommend starting with a tablecloth and full china set. Try a plastic glass of water, a cloth napkin, and a water-tolerant carpet. If you so choose, you can subsequently work your way up to bigger and better things.

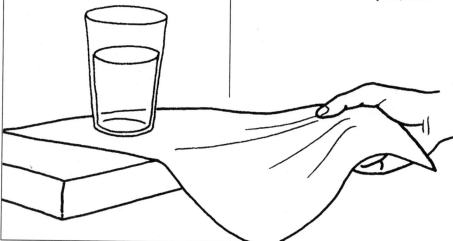

1 Drape a napkin over the edge of a table. Set a glass on one corner of the napkin about 1-2 inches from the border.

2 Grasp the napkin firmly. Pull it swiftly and surely out from under the glass. Don't jerk it hard, but not too soft, either—if you hesitate, you're lost.

3 If you do it right, the glass will remain on the table and not a drop will spill. If you do it wrong, at least you'll have a napkin in hand to blot up the water.

STRENGTH TRICKS

Do bullies taunt you? Do they kick sand in your face? It doesn't have to be that way.

With our simple plan, you can out-power the powerful. Best of all, there's nothing to write away for, no heavy lifting, no exotic diets, no exercises. Just basic physics, psychology, and good old-fashioned trickery.

After all, why settle for people thinking you're a 98-pound *weakling*? Why not trick 'em into thinking that you're a 98-pound *dynamo*?

Rip the Napkin

This is a good after-dinner trick. All you need is a good-quality paper napkin and a glass of water.

1 Take the napkin and roll it tightly into a rope. Challenge your friends to grab the two ends and tear it in half.

2 Odds are no-body can tear the napkin down the middle (don't let them tear a lit-tle off one end and claim they won).

3 As your friends strug-gle one after an-other to tear the napkin, dip your fingers casually into your water glass.

4 When you're handed the napkin take it in its center, allowing your fingers to wet the paper. Grip both ends, pretend to struggle, and then pull—it'll tear easily.

FISTICUFFS

This one is especially gratifying if you're with somebody much bigger than yourself.

1 Challenge your strong friend to stand with arms extended, one fist on top of the other. To win, your friend must keep the two fists together. You win if you can separate them.

2 Make sure your friend is ready. Encourage him or her to push hard, fist against fist.

3 Step forward deliberately, confidently. Look into your friend's eyes. Put your index fingers on the back of each fist, and suddenly push sideways in opposite directions. Because all of your friend's strength is directed up and down, and because

good leverage is hard to maintain with arms extended, you will have no trouble dislodging the hands.

4 If you want to add to your friend's humiliation, reverse the contest, offering a chance to separate your fists.

5 Here's how to win. It requires no great strength, just a little stealth. As you put your hands to-

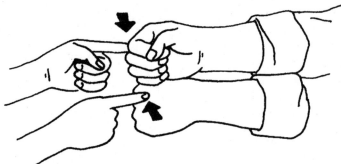

gether, sneak the thumb of your lower hand into the fist of your upper hand. Hang on tight and nothing but a knife can separate them!

NOT AN EASY PICKUP

This is a baffling trick that astounded vaudeville audiences at the turn of the century. A woman was billed as "The Girl You Cannot Lift," and she was able to live up to the name, supposedly by "willing" herself to gain weight.

Frankly, even knowing how she did her trick, we are still astounded. We haven't been able to figure out how or why it works. Maybe you can.

1 Announce that, at will, you can make yourself so heavy that you can't be lifted.

2 Pick a strong volunteer from the audience. Allow him or her to pick you up once and then set you down.

3 Announce that you are going to get heavy now, and that you are going to "drain the strength" of your volunteer.

4 Look your volunteer in the eye while he or she places hands at your waist to lift again. Place your right forefinger against the side of your volunteer's neck and your left hand on top of your volunteer's right wrist. Apply pressure to both spots at the same time.

5 Your volunteer won't be able to get you off the ground.

ASSORTED & SUNDRY

Odd Lots & Leftovers

There are certain tricks, stunts, and activities we ran across in our research that we didn't want to leave out but that didn't fit any of our existing categories.

After all, where could we fit fried marbles? Or a chain whittled from a single block of wood? Or the mysterious jumping rubber band?

This category, *Assorted & Sundry*, is intended to maintain the illusion of a comforting, unifying structure in this book. It is meant to hide from you the chaos that in reality seethes under the surface of this book and *everything*, ever threatening to spin dangerously out of control.

WHITTLE A CHAIN

Whittling has been a therapeutic method of relaxation for centuries. It costs nothing but time and patience, and it's fun in a slow, rural sort of way. Carve a chain from a single block of wood? It can be done.

1 For a three-link chain, a piece of basswood that's 1¹/₂ inches wide and 6 inches long is good. Make sure your knife is sharp, and be careful.

2 Take a pencil and draw guidelines as pictured, on all six sides of the board.

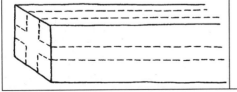

3 Begin cutting away the corner areas. Patiently slice a little at a time, or you'll split the wood. A good sharp knife and a meditative attitude will help a lot.

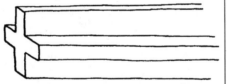

4 You'll have a cross-shaped block six inches long. Take your pencil and draw the two end links butted together and 3 inches long (as pictured above right). Draw the middle link centered on the "arms" of the cross, also 3 inches long.

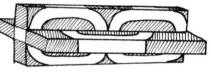

5 Start patiently whittling away the wood that doesn't belong to any of the links (dark areas, above). Eventually the links will become individual pieces, linked but hanging free.

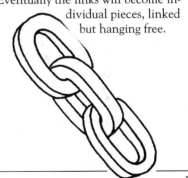

PLASTIC-CUP PHONE

This is an updated version of the classic tin can phone. We suggest using two "disposable" clear plastic cups instead of cans because they transmit sound better. You can even make the sound go around corners, making this a nifty intercom. When we figure out how to connect it to your personal computer and use it as a modem, we'll let you know.

1 Hold a nail with pliers, heat it up over a candle or stove, and use it to melt a small hole in the bottom of each cup.

2 Put a long string through the hole of one cup and tie a big knot. Do the same on the other end with your other cup.

3 You and your friend can now pull the string taut and start talking. The sound will travel through the string and vibrate the plastic cup on the other end.

4 Here's a way to be able to talk around corners: Normally, you have to send sound in a straight line, be-

cause contact with anything will stop the string from vibrating. But you can turn a corner if you tie a thread to the string and attach it to the far side of the door-frame.

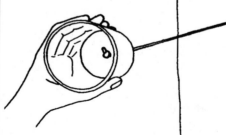
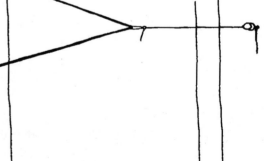

JUMPING RUBBER BAND

Here's what happens: You loop a rubber band over your first and second fingers. You snap it, and before your eyes, it jumps to your third and fourth fingers.

1 Show a rubber band looped over the first and second finger of your right hand.

2 Say: "I'm going to snap this rubber band twice. Watch what happens."

3 Pull the rubber band toward you with your left hand, and curl your right hand into a loose fist. Snap the rubber band so it hits gently into your fist. Open your fist. Nothing has changed; the rubber band is still in the same place. Say: "That's once."

4 Curl your hand again. This time, snap the rubber band so it lands across all four of your right hand's fingernails.

5 Open your fist. The rubber band instantaneously jumps from your first two fingers to your last two, in front of your friends' eyes.

6 Tell your friends you'll make it impossible this time. After putting the first rubber band on your first two fingers, take another and twist figure 8s across the top of the finger.

7 Do the trick again. Amazingly, it'll work just fine.

Jumping Paperclip

This variation requires two identical rubber bands and a paperclip.

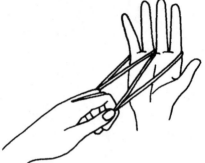

1 Loop the paperclip onto one of the rubber bands. Put it over your first two fingers. Take the other rubber band and put it on your last two fingers.

2 Tell your friends that you're going to make the paperclip instantly jump from the one rubber band to the other.

3 When you make a fist, snap both rubber bands onto your fingernails.

4 Open your hand. Your two rubber bands have instantaneously exchanged positions, but to the viewers, it looks like they stayed still and the paperclip suddenly jumped.

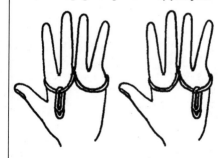

SNAPPING PEN CAP

1 Find one of those cheap ballpoint pens that have a tapered, removable plastic cap. Stick a little piece of a rubber band into the cap.

2 Tell your friend: "You know, I've always had a problem with these pens. The caps are always falling off, and then you can't put the pens into your pocket or briefcase without creating a problem."

3 Continue on: "So anyway, one day I got really mad because the cap slipped off and I ended up with ink all over my clothes. So I actually called the company that makes them. The president of the company came on and she apologized. She promised she'd send me a new prototype design that solves the problem. The next morning, I got an overnight package with this pen in it."

4 You explain that they fixed the problem with a little elastic thing that hooks onto the point. "If the cap gets loose, look what happens." Pulling the cap mostly off the pen, you let go and the cap snaps back into place.

5 What your friend doesn't know is that you're actually squeezing the cap and that it's really the pressure from your fingers that makes the cap snap back onto the pen.

6 Offer to let your friend try. It won't work, of course. Finally, shake the cap and let the rubber band fall out. Assure your friend several times that you're not angry about the broken pen (this is much more devastating than acting mad).

7 Put the rubber band back in, fiddle with it, "fix" it, and show that it works again. If you're a sadist, you'll offer to let your friend try it again . . .

FRIED MARBLES

Fried marbles? They were a fad for a while—about six weeks—in the middle of the 1960s, in roughly the same time frame as macrame, decoupage, and tie-dyed T-shirts. They were hoarded as is, or as quasi-semi-precious gems on pins, earrings, bracelets, and necklaces.

But unlike most 6-week fads from the 1960s, fried marbles have not, at this writing, come back in style. In fact, most people we've talked to don't even know what they are.

That's too bad, because they were great psychedelic fun—clear marbles shattered internally so they reflect and refract light in all directions. Fry up a batch: it might be the start of a new retro fashion trend.

1 Get a dozen or two transparent glass marbles of any light color (not "cat's eyes").

2 Put them in a clean skillet that can take a lot of heat. Cast iron is the best.

3 Put the skillet on the stove and turn the heat up as high as it can go. The pan is going to get *very* hot, so wear an oven mitt or two.

4 Heat the marbles at high for about ten minutes, stirring occasionally with a wooden spoon. They won't melt, just get good and hot.

5 Meanwhile, fill a metal pan with water and plenty of ice.

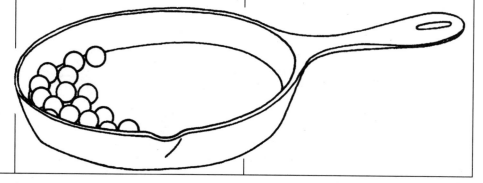

8 Wait for half a minute to make sure they are fully cool. Dry them off and admire your handiwork. They should be intact with their in-sides shattered into dozens of little light-bending facets like diamonds.

9 But if at first you don't succeed, then fry, fry again.

6 When the marbles are sizzling hot, turn off the heat and lift the pan carefully from the stove.

7 Pour the marbles from the skillet into the ice water, a few at a time. You'll notice that as soon as they hit the water, they crack inside.

GROOVY VIDEO LIGHT SHOW

While we're flashing back to the groovy 1960s, here's a hi-tech trick that will give your own moving mandala light show. All you need is a video camera and a television set.

1 Read your manual or bumble around and figure out how to connect your video camera to your TV in such a way that you get a "live" picture from your camera. This is usually pretty easy with the cords that came with the camera, although in some cases you might need to run down to your local electronics store.

2 With some cameras you have to put the camera on STANDBY or RECORD to see the picture (you might want to record anyway for viewing later). Sit directly in front of the TV with the camera on your lap. It actually helps if something is reflecting on the screen like a window

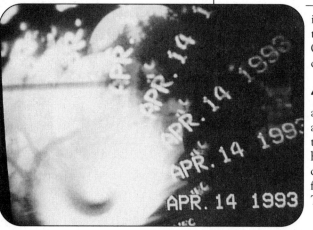

or a light or a candle flame.

3 Aim the camera at the center of the TV screen and tilt it slightly to one side. Zoom slowly in and out —suddenly the screen image will look like the backdrop for a Grateful Dead free concert, circa 1967.

4 Experiment with zooming, tilting, and changing the hue and brightness settings. Waving your hands in front of the camera brings new effects. *Far-out, man! Too much! Groooovy!*